RAILWAYS IN
SOUTH YORKSHIRE

C. T. Goode

First edition published by the Dalesman Publishing Company Ltd. in 1975.
This second, revised edition published by the author in 1990.
© C. T. Goode, 1990

ISBN 0 870313 07 0
72 Woodland Drive, Anlaby, Hull. HU10 7HX.

Designed, Printed and Bound by
Swannack, Brown & Co. Ltd.,
13a Anlaby Road, Hull.

Contents

Introduction

Not too much has been written about the railways of South Yorkshire, apart from the main line through Doncaster which everyone knows, possibly because it has been felt by many that the countryside through which they pass is of no great beauty or interest. Nothing could be further from the truth, for though black industry is to be found in profusion, which may at times reveal a quite surprising charm of its own, there are places where nature appears in her best guise.

I was fortunate in being brought up in the area at a time when it was possible as a boy to wander the roads which were, in wartime, relatively free of today's largely purposeless traffic, and see the railways in action set in this pleasant part of the country. The lines always blended well with the landscape, the little line to Sprotborough and Denaby seeming to enhance the scene with its bridges and cuttings tailor-made to fit the infrequent trains. Nothing more splendid could be witnessed than the sight and sound of a Great Central 4-6-0 getting away from Doncaster on the evening fish, usually to time and roaring away, a black column of smoke rising high into the air as the fireman could be seen frantically shovelling coal in the glare of the open firehole. An 04 would linger lazily at some home signal, the only activity being the sudden movement of the crew on the footplate, twiddling around somewhere inside behind the cab side, after which the engine would start to make contented gurgling and singing noises, both men now looking over the cab handrail—a little apprehensive, I always thought—until a jet of hot water and steam came out of a pipe somewhere below and peace descended again. The Dearne Valley push and pull train would enter the scene surreptitiously from Denaby, cross the viaduct to Edlington and return again, perhaps never seeing a passenger. Nor did the signalman at Yorkshire Main Sidings ever see the train, as the single line token was dealt with by a machine at a distance and the whole transaction assumed ghostly proportions.

I am in a way grateful to myself for writing this book, because it has provided me with an excuse to set out in instalments and re-visit all the locations covered, often a sad business as so much has vanished for ever, especially on the Hull and Barnsley scene. Elsewhere the picture is brighter, certainly on the old GCR route to Humberside. I would like to acknowledge with gratitude the kind assistance given to me by the Earl of Scarbrough, the Rt. Hon. Viscount Lumley, in making available material on the negotiations between Sandbeck and the South Yorkshire Joint Committee; also to thank Mr. D. Franks for his assistance with material and kind encouragement. Finally, I would offer thanks to Messrs. W. Ashton, G. S. Atkinson and J. P. R. Bennett, and all those railwaymen present and retired I have met in the course of my meanderings, without whom such a task would never have been completed.

A revision was called for and as far as possible this has been done. The reinstatement of small stations is very welcome, though recession in the coal industry, once almost the sole reason for many of the lines dealt with, has inflicted a heavy blow to the railway map. My apologies to readers who may find their favourite 'bits' missing. The great problem in compiling a work of this type is in judging what to leave out, or to emphasise.

C. Tony Goode B.A,
Anlaby, Hull. 1990.

Abbreviations used in the text:-

DV	Dearne Valley Railway.
GC	Great Central Railway.
GE	Great Eastern Railway.
GN	Great Northern Railway.
GW	Great Western Railway.
H&B	Hull and Barnsley Railway.
L&Y	Lancashire & Yorkshire Railway.
LD&EC	Lancashire, Derbyshire and East Coast Railway.
LMS	London, Midland and Scottish Railway.
LNER	London and North Eastern Railway.
LNW	London and North Western Railway.
Mid.	Midland Railway.
MS&L	Manchester, Sheffield and Lincolnshire Railway.
NE	North Eastern Railway.
NM	North Midland Railway.
S&K Jt	Swinton and Knottingley Joint Railway.
S&R	Sheffield and Rotherham Railway.
SYJ	South Yorkshire Joint Railway.
SY	South Yorkshire Railway.
WR&G	West Riding and Grimsby Railway.

Chapter One. The Railway comes to Sheffield. . .

Sheffield did not obtain a railway as soon as it would have liked, for George Stephenson surveyed the course of the great North Midland Railway to pass to the east of that city from Derby to Leeds (Hunslet Lane) via Chesterfield and Rotherham. The construction of the line began in February 1837 without any great difficulties, except those inherent in boring seven tunnels, including the lengthy one at Clay Cross. The prime reason for avoiding Sheffield was that a more easily graded route might be followed, generally along the valleys of rivers—seven again to match the number of tunnels. The grading of the line was beautifully executed, and the ruling incline was 1 in 130. Clay Cross marked the summit of the line at 360ft.; from here the line falls by easy stages to river level at Wath-on-Dearne and then rises and falls over a route beset by subsidence, to Leeds. The section from Derby to Rotherham (Masborough) was opened in May 1840, the rest of the run to Leeds following it in July of the same year. The ceremonies were intensive, as befitted the spirit of the times, and the first train from Leeds left Hunslet Lane at eight o'clock with two engines and 36 vehicles (no cause for alarm as they were all light four wheelers). Rather cleverly, it was arranged that George Hudson's York and North Midland line from York which joined the NM at Altofts should open on the same day, so that a train belonging to that company would be able to follow the first train to Derby, arriving shortly after one o'clock. Thus it was now possible to make the railway journey from London to York. Six trains were provided between Derby and Leeds in each direction at a return fare of 24s. for the four hour run.

How then, was Sheffield placed in view of the tremendous new rail activity on its eastern side? The major obstacle facing Stephenson was the barrier of hills to the south of the city, and the engineer in his wisdom could only offer an outlet to the north-east, along the Don valley to Rotherham following a reasonably graded route free of problems apart from some low viaducts. The line was authorised by an Act of 4th July, 1836, and opened on 31st October, 1838. It ran for over five miles from the Wicker station (later to become an LMS goods depot), named after the adjacent well-known local thorough-fare, not far from the Victoria station, and then through places which belie their names—Brightside and Meadow Hall—before running due east to a terminus at Westgate in Rotherham. Just before the run into Westgate spurs were built south and north from Holmes junction, and thus through running could be readily indulged in. So, on the great opening day of 11th May, 1840, the line ran a train from the Wicker station with through coaches for Derby which were transferred to the North Midland Railway at Masborough.

Sheffield remained cut off from the south until 1st February, 1870, when the direct line from Chesterfield via Dronfield and Bradway tunnel (1 mile 267yds.) was opened. Now it was possible to run services from St. Pancras and Derby via Sheffield and its fine new station, and round the north spur at Holmes junction into the Masborough station, now called Rotherham. As if to sustain the memory of the old S&R a certain number of local trains continued to run to Rotherham (Westgate) terminus until the closure of that station on 4th October, 1952. The last train to leave was the 5.28p.m. with Driver Gill and Fireman Dalton of Hasland shed. Of the new Midland station, the *Railway News* of the day said: "The building is of rock faced wall stone, tool dressed, the style of architecture being Grecian with Gothic headings." The reporter mentioned 79 passenger trains using the station even at that time, six of them to London. Nowadays almost all the passenger trains, apart from certain holiday workings which can avoid Sheffield, serve the city, and an interesting service which followed virtually the old S&R route to Holmes junction and then took the spur to Masborough South to reach Chesterfield via Treeton was withdrawn on 5th July, 1954.

On the NM direct line from Chesterfield to Rotherham a fair amount of heavy freight is carried, the stations at Whittington, Barrow Hill and Eckington being closed in 1952, 1954 and 1951 respectively. Killamarsh was served by three stations (the NM one closing in 1954), as the Rother valley at this point carries the routes of three companies, namely the Midland, the GCR extension to Marylebone and that of the Lancashire, Derbyshire and East Coast company from Shirebrook North, opened in 1898. Nearby, a complex interchange of lines takes place, due mainly to the LD&EC jockeying for position at the approach to Sheffield, which it reached as a guest of the Midland and via the Sheffield District Railway from Treeton junction to Brightside. This latter line was opened in May 1900 with trains of LD&EC stock running to Beighton junction and eventually to Langwith. Midland engines were used and the service lasted until 1939. Woodhouse Mill (closed in 1952) and Treeton (1951) occur next in succession before Masborough South junction is reached. After crossing the line to Westgate beneath the eastern leg of the triangle Rotherham station comes into view.

From Tapton junction where the original NM left to the north-east, the 1870 line to Sheffield runs through the site of the station at Sheepbridge and Dronfield, with the site of Unstone in between, to enter Bradway tunnel, after which comes the triangular junction with the Hope valley line to Chinley of 1893, and the adjacent bore of Totley tunnel (3 miles 950 yds.). The run down into Sheffield took in four suburban stations, all originally served by four tracks, including Dore and Totely which leads a precarious existence on the Paytrain route to Manchester (Piccadilly).

Northwards from Sheffield the NM line passes through a district which was at times so full of industrial dross that it became quite attractive in a perverse way. On through Rotherham it reaches Parkgate & Rawmarsh (surely one of the most squalidly placed of all stations) and Swinton with the GC line to Mexborough running parallel on the right. Swinton junction sent a spur down to the GC, round which went the first Midland trains to Doncaster via the South Yorkshire Railway in November 1849. After a break due to the last war the Sheffield (Midland) to Doncaster service was reinstated, running to Hull and indeed at times through to Manchester (Piccadilly) via a new link between the GC and Midland at Aldwarke junction and thence by way of the Hope valley line. At the time of writing the latest thinking has the original connection from the MR to the GC at Swinton renewed, replacing the transfer of traffic presently made at Aldwarke junction. Beyond Swinton the line traverses more industrial scenery, first of all at Wath-on-Dearne, where the Swinton and Knottingley Joint line with the NE of 1879 runs off northwards and where connection was made with the former SY on its run to Barnsley. At Wath the GC, H&B and Midland were all in close proximity. At Cudworth the NM was joined from the south-west by what was termed the Chapeltown loop, an alternative route from Brightside; then, north of what was originally a five platform station, the H&B main line came in on the east side. Connections between the H&B and the Midland were put in to allow through running between Hull Cannon Street and Sheffield in October 1905. From Cudworth a short branch led off to nearby Barnsley. Royston's large

7

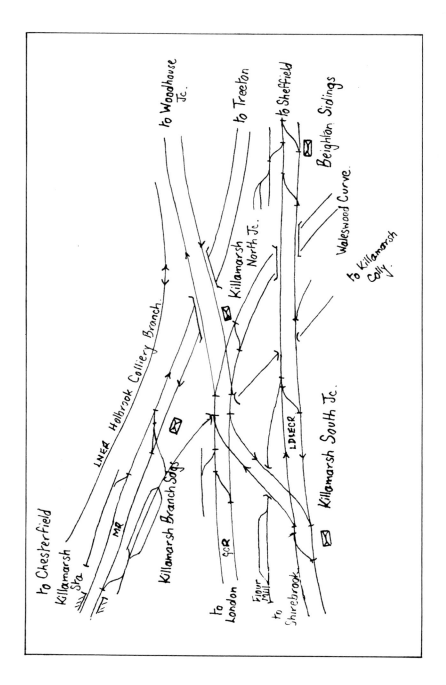

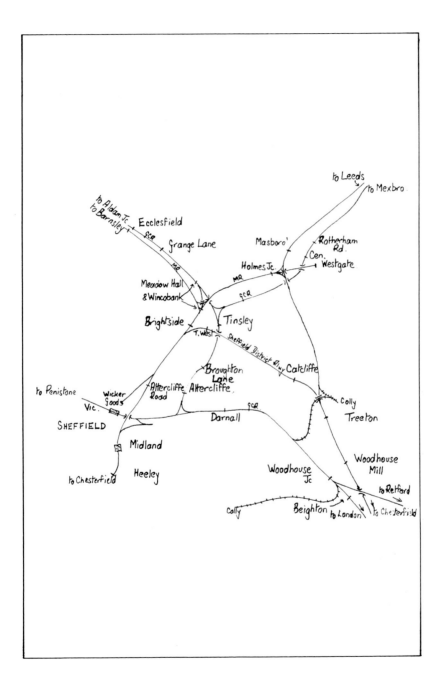

9

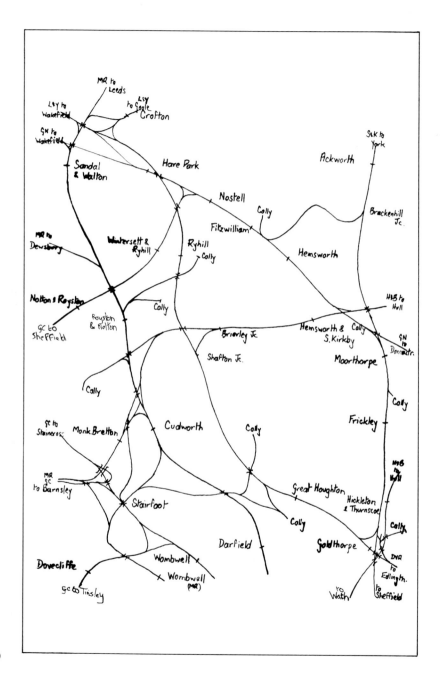

10

locomotive depot was on the east side of the line, while running away north-west was the line to Thornhill junction which was intended to put Bradford on the main line to London. This did attract a meagre service of trains worked by the L&Y between Bradford, Halifax and Sheffield, but it was eventually withdrawn in 1946. The NM had a tunnel at Chevet which was opened out into a 100ft. deep cutting in the twenties when the quadrupling of the tracks took place. A sketch will reveal a little of the complex nature of the junctions in the neighbourhood of Wakefield, spurs giving the NM access to both Kirkgate and Westgate stations in that city. Formerly, there was a station at Oakenshaw to serve Wakefield, near the Doncaster road. At the northern end of Oakenshaw cutting the line is joined by the L&Y route from the west, at Goose Hill junction, from which point the two companies ran to Normanton, a vast island platform in the style of Trent with ample bays at each end. After the introduction of dining cars, Normanton lost much of its status as a refreshment stop where good meals were served with commendable promptitude. For a time the station building still survived in its original form, one suspects with the old dining rooms somewhere about the place, though humbled to Paytrain status. At Altofts just north of here traffic passed on to the North Eastern. Today the old North Midland lines within the area covered do a fair business, and an hour spent at somewhere like Sheffield on a summer Saturday can be quite rewarding as far as seeing operating is concerned.

George Dow in the first of his three volume history of the Great Central Railway gives many details of the trials, tribulations and triumphs attending the birth of the line across the Pennines to Manchester. This was known firstly as the Sheffield, Ashton-under-Lyne and Manchester, and then as the Manchester, Sheffield and Lincolnshire, to become at the turn of the century the Great Central on completion of the last main line to reach London. Woodhead tunnel had not been completed and road vehicles had to be provided to close the gap when the first train left Bridgehouses (only a temporary terminus, later a goods depot) in Sheffield at 9.25 a.m. on 14th July, 1845. Trains left Bridgehouses to what might be considered a very modern looking timetable, at 7.25 and 9.25 a.m., 12.25, 4.25 and 5.25 p.m., with four trains on Sundays and an equal number the other way to a more ragged looking set of departure times. There were five intermediate stations in Yorkshire at Wadsley Bridge, Oughty Bridge, Deepcar, Wortley and Penistone. Woodhead tunnel was opened on 22nd December, 1845, a special train of 20 vehicles leaving at 10.5 a.m. drawn by two locomotives.

From Bridgehouses construction continued eastwards into Sheffield, a difficult job as the line had to be carried at a high level over the Don on the Wicker arches for 660 yds. with a road span of 72 ft. Adjacent was the Victoria station and hotel, also on embankment with a long approach road from the south and a choice of steps or a lift (1 d.) down to the Wicker, a precarious path for old ladies. Without too much ado the station was opened on 15th September, 1851, a Plain Jane of a place, very unpretentious and functional. If one must seek distinguishing features, then perhaps the overall glass roof with a length of 400ft. might raise an eyebrow. A contemporary newspaper account is worth quoting: "The arrangements of the station will be very complete for excluding from it the crowds of idlers who are often a great impediment to business. The places of exit will be closed by sliding gates which will be opened only when a train arrives. Besides this, the platform will be divided longitudinally by an iron railing, with sliding gates at intervals. Through these gates only persons who have tickets will pass. Friends who go to see them depart will remain on the outer side of the railing, sufficently near to utter their last adieus, without impeding the loading of the carriages. These arrangements are expected to conduce greatly to the orderly and quick despatch of the business of the station".

The line followed an undulating course out to Woodburn junction, picking up first a connection from the Midland at Nunnery, now used to transfer the diesel units which ran through the closed Victoria—where the "last adieus" have been well and truly said—and into the Midland station by reversing at this point. Next comes the southern arm of a triangular junction opened in 1861, the point where the Mexborough line departs. At the east end of the triangle was the Handsworth tunnel of 374yds., opened out during widening in 1912, and south of the line was the important steam shed of Darnall. At Woodhouse junction the new extension to London went off; opened in March 1899, this was always known to the older GC men as "the branch". At Waleswood a spur was put in to allow south to east running to take place in the direction of Shireoaks, Worksop and Retford. A short way south on the new line to Marylebone was Beighton junction and station, where the interchange with the Midland and the LD&EC companies took place.

Chapter Two. . . . and to Barnsley

The time has now come to bring into the picture one of the most individual and possibly the most eccentric of railways ever to operate in this country, the South Yorkshire Railway, and with it to bring Barnsley into the reckoning, since the SY provided a passenger service to that town from 1851, the line running via Ardsley to Doncaster, with branches to Worsborough at Aldam junction and a goods line to Elsecar. The first section of line was opened from Doncaster to Swinton in November 1849 in inclement weather which thwarted efforts to get things moving in time for the September races of that year. A separate station was provided in Cherry Tree Lane south-west of the GN station in Doncaster, with a connection southwards and another north-wards to the major company. The personages assembled in the goods wagon propelled by the engine were suitably impressed, particularly by the "forbidding cutting" between Hexthorpe and Warmsworth which still makes an impact on the modern traveller riding up front in the diesel units of today, its limestone sides coming down sheer to 70 feet or so. At Conisbrough is the Rainbow bridge over the Don, then a short tunnel out of which the traveller bursts forth to see the splendid view of Conisbrough castle with its hexagonal keep crowning its own hill. The present day view is enhanced by the sweep of the Dearne Valley Railway viaduct which runs across the valley and is now sadly abandoned. Conisbrough and Mexborough each have their own stations, both having originally had sites some way to the east of their present positions. Both also had until recently three platforms simply formed by making one side an island. Mexborough station looks slightly self-conscious today, having been recently cleaned of its ancient layer of steam-era grime. Affixed to the main building is the polished plaque in memory of the company's servants who fell in the Great War. There were originally stations at Hexthorpe and at Sprotborough, one under the Greenfield Lane bridge, the other at Mill Lane bridge in a ridiculous position in the aforementioned deep cutting which was available to the athletic passenger willing to cope with 66 steps and also stand on a platform about one foot wide! The booking office here was a tarred wooden lean-to structure which survived until about 1945 as a platelayers' lobby. Today the lobby has gone, though the bricked-up space can be seen from a train. The station cottages still exist at road level on the west side of the bridge.

The SY made connection with the Midland at Swinton, the latter company swiftly supplying the service using their own locomotives and carriages. The first departures from Doncaster were at 9.30 a.m., 1 p.m., 4.30 p.m. XP and at 7 p.m., while from Sheffield Wicker trains left at 8 a.m., 11.10 a.m., 2.15 p.m. and 5.45 p.m. In July 1851 the extension from Swinton to Barnsley was opened, the GN providing four trains daily from Doncaster which called at Wath, Wombwell and Ardsley (later named Stairfoot to avoid confusion with the other Ardsley near Wakefield). In GC days this section of line was expanded into four tracks linked with the important concentration yard on the south side at Wath opened in 1907. Mexborough has waxed and waned in importance, and had at one time six signal boxes to control the various junctions. From Mexborough a line led south to give the SY, which was absorbed into the MS&L in 1864, an independant route via Kilnhurst, Parkgate, Rotherham Road, Rotherham, Tinsley, Broughton Lane and Attercliffe to Sheffield Victoria. Near Kilnhurst, Thrybergh junction gave access eastwards to the Silverwood branch. Rotherham Road appeared to serve nowhere in particular apart from a tram depot, and was next to a nasty little canal swing bridge which demanded a heavy speed restriction at all times and even today exerts its influence by flooding the line. Rotherham Central was gloomy and had staggered platforms. A new station was opened here on the site of the old one in the last three years, with parallel platforms, smart covered footbridges and a booking office with a clock tower. Tinsley was beset by steel works and lay at the southern end of a triangle, the line from this running north-west being the original route by which SY trains reached Sheffield from Barnsley, using the Midland line to Wicker station. Present day Doncaster to Sheffield services ran via Mexborough to a new scissors junction at Aldwarke, where they then went Midland. The advent of the new Rotherham Central brought stopping trains along the old GC line, however, to regain the Midland route by way of a single line round Booth's scrapyard to Holmes junction. Trains not calling at Rotherham ran along the MR to Aldwarke junction through the site of the redundant Masborough station. The remainder of the 1871 route is left as goods only, thus depriving the passenger of some splendid industrial scenery and of the chance of passing the quaintly named Ickles signal box, now, alas no more.

The line from Aldam junction to the Midland near Tinsley was opened in 1854, Barnsley to Sheffield trains having to reverse at the junction which faced the wrong way. Stations were at Smithley, High Royds, Birdwell, Westwood, Chapeltown, Ecclesfield, Grange Lane and Meadow Hall. Noteworthy are Birdwell and Grange Lane, both having very old signal boxes. The line has now no passenger trains, but serves the large complex of Newton, Chambers LTD. (Izal).

The MS&L entered Barnsley from the west in 1859, with a branch from Penistone via Silkstone, Dodworth and Summer Lane to a station build jointly with the L&Y which was later known as Exchange. The L&Y reached Barnsley via Darton from Wakefield along a branch undistinguished apart from some lively gradients and the Woolley tunnel, or rather tunnels, between Criggle-

Conisbrough Station in its original form, looking west.   *C.T. Goode*

stone and Haigh, there being separate bores at a fair distance from each other for some 1,745 yd. Today the line is part of the modern route from Leeds to Sheffield via Wakefield. The Penistone branch fell quite steeply into Barnsley with a ruling gradient of 1 in 100 and a keen 1 in 50 at the Exchange station end. Probably due to the adverse gradients the line, though a through one between Doncaster and Manchester, was not fully exploited for long distance trains, its use being confirmed largely to Penistone to Cleethorpes stopping trains which took four hours for the 84 miles, or the more localised workings such as the rather jolly Penistone to Doncaster train. This used to run in at about 7 o'clock made up of three elderly GC coaches and a C14 4-4-2 tank (usually 67411 or 67434) with a string of milk tankers at its tail from the Co-op Dairy at Summer Lane. The return working booked for 9.30 p.m. would often be held to connect with the arrival of the Yorkshire Pullman from London, particularly if the MP for Barnsley was on board, in which case the old engine would belt away from Doncaster in fine style and showers of hot cinders. Until recently a night newspaper train ran via Penistone eastwards from Manchester, while from time to time certain holiday trains for Blackpool not requiring to stop at Sheffield would use the line. Sheffield-Huddersfield trains now run the gauntlet of a scenic route via Barnsley and Penistone, with a reopened station at Dodworth.

With the increase in traffic the MS&L found it necessary to extend the goods branch from Worsborough (Moor End) further westwards to link up with the existing route from Barnsley to Penistone at Silkstone. This extension was opened in 1880 and remained a mineral route for the whole of its life, being the abode of the LNER's only Garratt locomotive No. 2395 which, when not out of service on Mexborough shed with steam pipe troubles, spent its time assisting coal trains up the bank on the line. With Manchester to Sheffield electrification this line was included in the stretch down to Wath yard.

Exchange station in Barnsley was a humble affair on a cramped site, with a single platform only on the down side and a locomotive shed occupying the other. The L&Y and the MS&L (GC) used the station jointly until the Midland built their own superior structure on an embankment nearby, calling it Court House and opening it in 1870. The MS&L willingly paid for half the cost of its construction in order to be able to use it and get out of Exchange which was not doing their image any good. Contemporary accounts have it as a dreadful place. Today it has been suitably and pleasantly improved, with an additional up platform. The Midland built a branch from Cudworth to Court House, and to gain access to this station the MS&L ran over new junctions at Quarry and West, and thence over the new embankment to the station with its all-over roof and bay at the west end. Beyond, at Court House junction, the MS&L was able to rejoin its original route. Today the irony of fate is perhaps in evidence as Court House station has vanished and all trains use Exchange, taking a new southern spur from Jumble Lane crossing up to the ex-Midland line which eliminates two junctions at a stroke. Possibly the most interesting engineering feature of the lines in the Barnsley area was the long 1,000ft. viaduct on the Midland branch to Cudworth, with nine iron piers and three stone ones. For a time Ivatt 2-6-2T No. 41281 of Royston shed worked the push and pull service on the branch. Barnsley GC shed was almost entirely given over to tank engines of Classes C13 and 14, N5s, J11 0-6-0s and 04 and Q4 tender engines, all stemming from the old Great Central. Before leaving Barnsley mention should be made of the passenger service from Exchange to Wakefield via Nostell, a GC venture which vanished in the early thirties.

Chapter Three. Doncaster Station and "The Plant"

Before we pursue the extended course of the SY beyond Doncaster to the north and east, it is perhaps opportune to mention at this point the arrival of the Great Northern railway in the town, which completely transformed its character, both in its size and in the nature of its industry. The GN reached Doncaster in 1849 by way of its present route through Retford which roughly follows the Great North Road. The original proposal specified a line by way of Lincoln, Gainsborough and Selby, which excluded Doncaster altogether; however, this idea was vigorously opposed by Mr. Edmund Beckett Denison, the local Member of Parliament who later became chairman of the GN. Thus, the headquarters of the company came to be in an ideally situated geographical position for the locomotive and carriage works, known locally as "the Plant", which are sited to the west of the station and are approached by means of a lengthy footbridge at the south end of the platforms. Peterborough was the other favourite for the housing of the workshops, but Doncaster won the day and in 1853 the present works was erected for £50,000, the wagon, dray and grease departments being situated on the Carrs some two miles nearer to London on the down side of the line. The total acreage covered by the works was originally about 75, the locomotive and carriage departments employing

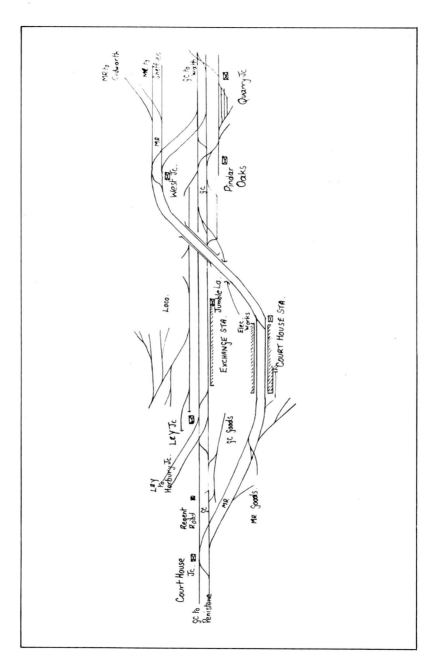

16

Worsborough Banker at Mexborough shed in 1939, Garratt type. The most powerful (and awkward) loco on the LNER.

about 4,000 men. The capacity of the locomotive shops as regards new construction, begun in 1867, was about 50 engines per year with a repair turnover of 600. In the early years of this century around 70 coaches were built yearly and, if one is really interested in the finer statistics, then the grease plant produced 800 tons annually and there were some sixty miles of sidings in the GN's Doncaster district.

The original station at Doncaster consisted of two platforms, each of 460ft. in length served by loops off the through running lines. At the south end by the up platform was a small engine shed. With the approach of the SY into the station a larger one was evolved having three main platforms, two as now, serving northbound trains each side of an island. There were also four bays, two at the south end of the up and two at the north end of the down platform. The longest platform was the western or outside of the down island at 380yds. The improved station was liberally provided with booking offices on both up and down sides respectively, each of the companies which ran to the station having its own facilities, though of course sharing the often rather cramped platforms. From the north came the NE from York and the L&Y from Knottingley via Shaftholme junction. The MS&L ran in from the Mexborough direction and Midland trains used the same route from Swinton. The GE came in from the south-east along the GN main line from Black Carr junction. Additionally, even the LNW gained a foothold for goods traffic by exercising its rights over the GN from Bottesford via Newark and running to a separate locomotive shed near to that of the premier company on its north side. Thus,

17

six separate concerns had an interest in the traffic generated by the town. Before nationalisation, some 19 signal boxes controlled operations in the area and for several miles south-east of the town there was much land available to fit in some most impressive goods yards, as at Decoy, named after the devices used to lure ducks on to the scene before shooting them, a typical sport in this marshy district. North of the station the operation was more cramped, due to the presence of the Great North Road, followed by the canal and the river Don. The road was crossed on the level by the double track at Frenchgate junction box prior to the first World War, and this must have been quite a position to man with the continuous through traffic, station and carriage works shunting movements all blocking from time to time an important road carrying heavy traffic. Add to this over 1,000 extra trains run for the typical four day September Race Week of the first decade of this century—a figure unbelievable but true—and one has some idea of the magnitude of operations. Over the canal the bottleneck branched three ways, the left line being the route to Leeds, that straight ahead to York, while that to the right was the GC continuation to Grimsby upon which NE trains approached from Thorne junction running from Hull.

The layout at Doncaster began to assume something like its present form in 1938 when extensive improvements were put in hand. As originally improved there was no island platform on the up side (facing the town), and passengers were able to walk on to this side from the street, gaining the other side by means of a covered footbridge. The major transformation was the conversion of the eastern side into an island, the new platform thus formed becoming No. 1. Access to all the platforms Nos. 1-8 was now by subway leading from a new covered concourse, the footbridge being dismantled. Also attended to was the bottleneck under the North Bridge, which replaced the level crossing about 1910. Capacity for adding an extra running line in each direction was in fact available as a couple of bridges used only for sidings flanked the up and down running lines and were virtually unemployed. It is surprising that no attention had been given to installing these relief lines earlier in the station's history. In 1924, however, the problem of the bottleneck had already become so acute that a long by-pass for the town, between Moss in the north and Bawtry to the south had been suggested, to be greeted by howls of derision by local business interests who feared for a loss of trade as a possible outcome of such a scheme. The improvements to the north of the station now meant that a train from the Hull direction or from Grimsby could run into the station at the same time as a train from York or Leeds, each approaching platforms 1 and 4 simultaneously, while a Leeds train could slip unobtrusively out of 8 without unduly worrying anything going off 5 to York or Hull. This did not prevent *Water Witch*, a Sentinel steam railcar on a run from the Hull direction, having an argument with a GC 4-4-0 as both tried to reach the station at the same time, and one suspects on the same line! Colour light signalling was installed at the station in December 1949, the new North and South cabins replacing "A", "B" and South boxes and the South Yorkshire, Frenchgate and Marshgate junctions, clearing away at a sweep several clusters of GN somersault signals and a fine gantry of 16 arms at Bridge junction. For some reason the old "C" cabin survived for a time to supervise shunting movements in the West Yard between the Plant and platform 8. The present-day layout also remains clumsy for through goods workings, freight from the south being easily routed either via the down main or by way of a choice of two loop lines through the West Yard area. Up freight working bound for the GN main line must clatter through the station, whereas

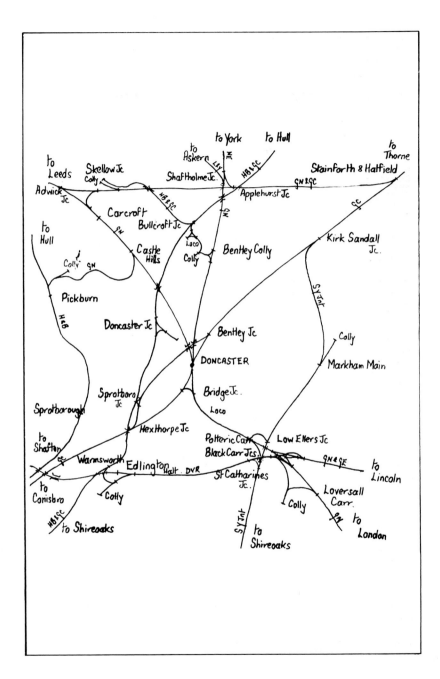

Class D6 No. 5874 at Doncaster on a Penistone train. C.T. Goode

Ex GC 4.6.0 No. 6099 leaves the Cattle Dock sidings at Doncaster with a short train of GN coaches. T. Rounthwaite

any traffic for the GC line has to be turned across, fouling the whole layout at the main end, to pass round to the west of the station. However, this arrangement does lessen the confusion which these trains would cause at the south end where, in any case, passenger workings for Sheffield off platform 3 have to find their way across the whole run of lines.

Train workings at Doncaster were always fascinating, and even today an hour spent on the platform usually yields some interesting happenings. The author spent many hours during and after the last war both on the station premises and on the nearby cattle dock in observing the pageant of steam power which passed to and fro. Taking the 1950 period as perhaps a notable one, every Saturday during the summer of that year saw no less than 380 arrivals or departures, plus the through workings non-stop, the total representing normal runs and not including extras. During the night time the parcels and newspapers would arrive and be dealt with, while in the season fruit would be reaching West Yard for sorting and forwarding by the van load, these bearing such names of origin as Tydd, Clenchwarton and Murrow, places which shook off rural peace for a brief span. Hull newspapers always went forward on the 4.3 a.m. from No. 6 bay. Constantly, non-stop trains would be passing up and down through the centre roads, while traffic was being dealt with at the platforms. Basically, the operating pattern at Doncaster would be divided into three "peaks", namely the morning "rush", an early afternoon period and one in the early evening. An outline of weekday departures at these periods will be of interest:

Time	Destination	Platform
7.42 a.m.	Sheffield	5
8.10 a.m.	Leeds	8 ex King's Cross
8.15 a.m.	York	5
8.16 a.m.	King's Cross	4 ex Leeds
8.30 a.m.	Sheffield	1
8.48 a.m.	King's Cross	4 ex Leeds
8.50 a.m.	Cleethorpes	5
9.00 a.m.	Hull	8
9.00 a.m.	Peterborough	2
12.15 p.m.	Leeds	5
12.30 p.m.	King's Cross	4 ex Ripon
12.50 p.m.	Leeds	6
12.51 p.m.	York	5 ex Colchester
12.57 p.m.	Hull	8 ex Liverpool (Cen)
1.05 p.m.	Barnsley	1
1.26 p.m.	Cleethorpes	5
5.45 p.m.	Leeds	6
6.19 p.m.	King's Cross	4 ex Hull and Leeds
6.20 p.m.	Hull	8 ex Sheffield (Vic)
6.25 p.m.	Peterborough	2
6.34 p.m.	Newcastle	5 ex King's Cross
6.42 p.m.	Leeds	8 ex King's Cross
6.55 p.m.	Sheffield	2
7.28 p.m.	Swindon	1 ex York
7.32 p.m.	Leeds	8 ex King's Cross
7.37 p.m.	Lincoln	4
7.40 p.m.	York	5

7.45 p.m.	Barnsley	4
7.56 p.m.	Hull	8 ex Liverpool (Cen)
8.23 p.m.	Harrogate	5 ex King's Cross (Pullman)
8.29 p.m.	Hull	5

A study of the departure times given will reveal one or two interesting points and a certain general consistency in platform allocation, northbound Leeds trains usually running into 8 in order to be clear of other northbound trains departing for elsewhere. Similarly No. 1 is so used, though wherever possible No. 4 (the present day No. 3) is utilised. At times of pressure two trains may be found nose to tail at any one of the through platforms, as these are long enough to admit two short sets of coaches. One advantage of the improvements of early days was that trains from the Sheffield direction could use No. 5 instead of being confined to No. 8 only. A function now almost forgotten at Doncaster was the dividing of a train from King's Cross into parts for Leeds and Hull, the Leeds portion usually leading and going out first, leaving the Hull portion of three or four coaches on No. 5 to await the arrival of the K3 2-6-0 or D49 4-4-0 to take them forward, usually at a spanking rate. The same of course happened in the southerly direction, the Hull portion arriving on No. 4, usually followed by the heavier Leeds train on No. 1. The engine of this latter portion, which would be going on to London with the working, would uncouple, run ahead and come down No. 4 to take up the Hull coaches (the Hull crew having hurried their locomotive off to the shed) and attach them to the head of the train, sometimes in a manner which greatly displeased the restaurant car staff tussling with the remains of breakfast in the pantry. This manoeuvre happened with the 10 a.m. out to King's Cross, and also with the Yorkshire Pullman later in the morning. The use of bay platforms has declined up to the present time, when only those at the north end are in regular use to house the diesel sets for Cleethorpes. With the closure of many intermediate stations and with the cessation of the Barnsley service the use of the short bays is virtually at an end. One of the most interesting trains was the York-Swindon through service which used to run each way via Doncaster before the 1939-45 war and brought the brown and yellow coaches of the GW to the station. In pre-war days a D9 4-4-0 would proudly bring in such a train at about 2.15 p.m., and then on it would go to Sheffield, the nameboards of the carriages sporting almost every major city en route from Aberdeen to Penzance. After the war the down train went via Church Fenton and Pontefract (Baghill), only the up service running via Doncaster, from where it departed at about 7.30 p.m. for Sheffield (Victoria), where reversal took place before the run to Nottingham and beyond as far as Swindon which was reached at midnight. The train conveyed much valuable nylon and tobacco traffic from Nottingham to the GW in sealed vans.

A further noteworthy train was the 7.42 a.m. to Sheffield, not in itself odd but only in the fact that it left from No. 5, the down platform, by a wrong line movement controlled by a miniature signal tucked under the canopy. The reason for this irregularity was a very important one, as the wagon shops express was in occupation of No. 4, always made up of a rake of 13 GN four-wheelers, plus one six-wheeler, all at one time in blue and latterly in a teak style. Some compartments were set aside and labelled for "ladies" and "foremen" and other selected staff. At the head would be a J52 0-6-0 tank with proud express headlamps, for the train was non-stop along the mainline for the 1¾ miles to the special halt for the works beside the down goods line. For some reason unknown the area was christened by the staff "Spike

Island", the train itself being "The Spike Island Flyer". The train was crewed by the wagon shops staff who worked the yard during the day and brought their colleagues back to Doncaster at the end of it, when it was stored in the West Yard for the night. The train provided a fine free ride, but the running was decidedly rough on the rigid wheelbase. The Carr Wagon Works were closed in the sixties, production being transferred to the Plant.

Fruit traffic has already been mentioned in connection with the West Yard; the other important commodities handled at Doncaster have always been coal, meat and fish, the latter being received from Hull and Grimsby and assembled into train loads such as the evening runs to Ardwick (Manchester) and to Nottingham via Tuxford, usually hauled in steam days by the B7 4-6-0s of the old GC, always strident and with voracious appetites for coal.

Needless to say, there was always a rich selection of motive power on view at the station with locomotives of almost every type appearing at some time or other, including guest appearances from the NE which sent in wheezing old war horses from Hull, the GE which covered services to Lincoln and beyond, and the Midland division of the LMS which maintained a token service into Doncaster from Sheffield (Midland) up to the outbreak of the 1939 war. Maroon coaches came in from the north, too, the L&Y running in rather shyly from Knottingley until the run was cut back during the war to the last station on the line, Askern, to save the use of the GN main line from Shaftholme junction. Doncaster shed housed about 200 steam locomotives, the principal performers being four A3 Pacifics and some 25 or so maids-of-all-work 2-6-2s, the V2s. The famous streamlined engines of class A4 were less frequently based there, though the big 4-6-4 engine No. 10000 spent its last days on the shed. For lighter duties, K3 2-6-0s and B1 4-6-0s abounded; one of the latter class, No. 1120, gained a bad reputation after failing at Broughton Lane with a crowded football special before an important fixture in 1950. Freight locomotives found at Doncaster included 02 and 04 2-8-0s, J6 and J39 0-6-0s and, for shunting, swarms of indigenous and breathy little J50 and J52 tank engines, as well as multifarious droppers-in of every type. There was never a turntable at the shed, engines being turned on a triangular layout to the east of the main building.

Mention has been left until last of the great event of the year, the St. Leger race week in September which, needless to say, is now only a shadow of its former self as far as railway activity is concerned, though the influx by motor coach increases each year. Years ago the order of the day was to clear all sidings in the area of traffic for the week, including those of the Plant works which were closed. Extra signal boxes were erected to increase the capacity of the line, and the life of the station proper was heightened by the strengthening of normal services through reliefs, duplicates and the like. The excursion trains were disposed of as follows:

L&Y and H&B to the Works carriage sidings.
NE and Midland to the down goods yard.
GN, GC and LNW trains to the Shakespeare sidings
(south end, east side).

Each passenger alighted on the trackside and was given a handbill which told him of the number and departure time of his train. In 1892 the GN alone ran 15 excursions from King's Cross at a day return rate of 12s. 6d., and on St. Leger Day in 1905 a total of no less than 89 excursions put in an appearance. Much of the September Race traffic was handled at St. James's Bridge station, the site of the SY's Cherry Lane terminus, set in the fork of the GN and GC routes at the south end of Doncaster with an approach ramp beloved by spotters leading down to it. The station, though not in use for much of the year, had a complete set of signs, was fully signalled and had a substantial "hill and dale" roof. Pre 1939 race traffic was still big business and the special operating manual for that year was 75 pages of carefully laid planning. Today its words are in some respects as fascinating as a good novel:-

"The Guards, Drivers and Firemen of Special trains to Doncaster must not leave their trains until they have been formed and placed ready for return and receive special permission from the inspector; they must be on duty and in charge of their respective trains one hour before the time of returning. Guards will be held responsible for seeing that roof and tail lamps on their trains, where required, are lighted half an hour before due to leave Doncaster in the evening, and be prepared with keys for lighting coaches fitted with incandescent and electric lamps. . . The signalman at Cadeby between 9.30 a.m. and 1.30 p.m. on each race day must telephone the departure and number of all Up trains to the Signalman at St. James's Jc. particulars of the trains terminating at St. James's Bridge station. . . Inspector Lister must instruct the Signalman at St. James's Bridge Jc. into which platform each incoming train is to be turned. . . Return tickets from Sheffield and intermediate stations to Doncaster issued by the LNER and LMS Companies will be available for return from Doncaster by either Company's trains. . . The Loco. Department will arrange for a Pilot to be at Barnsley Court House Jc. from 5 p.m. until the passing of the last Down Race Special on the four Race Days, to assist trains if necessary over the inclines".

On the preceding weekend horse box specials were run from Moreton-in-Marsh, Winchester, Newport Pagnell, Fenny Stratford, Newbury, Cheltenham, Winslow and Lambourne, an impressive list of almost all the places where the best winners come from. Typical of the normal race day arrivals was Tuesday, 5th September, the first day of the 1939 meeting:-

Arrivals at Central Station:
11.22 a.m. from Birmingham.
11.37 a.m. from Heeley.
11.52 a.m. from Hull.
12.09 p.m. from Sheffield.
12.17 p.m. from Liverpool Central.
(Restaurant Car: dep. 9.33 a.m.)
12.29 p.m. from Sheffield.
12.40 p.m. from Nottingham Vic.
12.57 p.m. from Wadsley Bridge.

Arrivals at St. James's Bridge:
10.49 a.m. from Dovecliffe.
10.54 a.m. from Sheffield.
11.05 a.m. from Deepcar.
11.16 a.m. from Sheffield.
11.26 a.m. from Wadsley Bridge.
11.55 a.m. from Sheffield.

Normal race days were the Tuesday, Thursday and Friday. The day of days was the St. Leger Day on the Wednesday, the event attracting very many people of all types who often travelled in groups organised by local clubs. Both the "Rose and Shamrock" of Altrincham, and the "Locomotive" of Northwich sent parties, while from Chester came groups from five hotels. The "Kitty Smiles" Outing Club came from Liverpool with 38 passengers who could afford to dine en route—and many more came. Many trains were made up of the oldest vehicles imaginable; even in 1949 6 wheelers put in a gaslit appearance on runs from Barnsley. To offer some idea of the pressure on the operating staff at this busy time, below is given the passing times of all trains at Hexthorpe junction on the Sheffield line some two miles outside the town,

24

the point where the trains from St. James's Bridge filtered into the main line from Doncaster Central. Add to the list a few trains of freight waiting to run off the "Avoiding Line" which comes in at this point, and the busy picture is complete.

Passenger workings passing Hexthorpe junction westbound, Wednesday, 6th September 1939.
All departures from St. James's Bridge, unless otherwise.
5.28 p.m. to Sheffield. Ordinary from Central.
5.41 p.m. to Sheffield.
5.44 p.m. to Penistone. Ordinary from Central.
5.49 p.m. to Manchester Central.
5.57 p.m. to Sheffield.
6.02 p.m. to Dovecliffe.
6.09 p.m. to Macclesfield.
6.13 p.m. to St. Helen's.
6.17 p.m. to Sheffield from Central.
6.20 p.m. to Rugby Central.
6.24 p.m. to Sheffield.
6.36 p.m. to Luton Midland.
6.40 p.m. to Barnsley.
6.44 p.m. to Liverpool Central.
6.48 p.m. to Hinckley.
6.52 p.m. to Deepcar.

"Deltic" No. D9003 crosses the canal bridges north of Doncaster with an Edinburgh - King's Cross express in August 1970.   T.G. Flinders

6.57 p.m. to Sheffield.
7.04 p.m. to Chester.
7.10 p.m. to Swindon. Ordinary from Central.
7.14 p.m. to Wadsley Bridge.
7.18 p.m. to Gloucester from Central.
7.22 p.m. to Heath.
7.29 p.m. to Sheffield Midland. Ordinary from Central.
7.36 p.m. to Chester.
7.41 p.m. to Sheffield.
7.45 p.m. to Liverpool Central. Ordinary from Central.
7.54 p.m. to Coventry from Central.
8.05 p.m. to Kidsgrove from Central.
8.15 p.m. to Heeley from Central.
9.07 p.m. to Wadsley Bridge from Central.
Due to the outbreak of war, the 1939 race extras never actually ran.

The first signal box out of Doncaster over the line to Thorne junction, Marshgate Goods, celebrated its centenary in 1973. Old it certainly looked and it was easily seen by any interested travellers using the north end of the station; however, the route it served ante-dates it by some twenty years, as the old SY projected its Barnsley line through the town out to Thorne and Keadby in 1855, and this was ready for passenger services in July 1856. The route followed was only loosely the one which is taken today, the station at Barnby Dun lying north-west of the later site, from which point the canal bank was followed to a station at Bramwith, north of the later WR&G structure. Stainforth station was also nearer the canal to the north, while at Thorne there was only one single station in the fork of the present Thorne junction, with a north spur to the canal side. However, east of Thorne the line of route opened in September 1859 followed the present level and ran by way of Medge Hall and Crowle to its wharf at Keadby, to which point the Barnsley coal was sent in 1860 for shipment to Grimsby. Thorne Old station was replaced by Thorne New three years later in 1859 when the route eastwards was opened.

In MS&L hands the section of line between Marshgate and Thorne was straightened out to its present form and was quadrupled as far as Kirton Lane. Today the line carries a healthy traffic, including freight off the NE Hull outlet via Goole. Stainforth remained much as in its final form with three platforms and a yard on each side of the line. Barnby Dun was closed about 1968, being too far away from the village and beset by a frequent bus service. Thorn junction, a big installation, was rationalised in 1971 and the box abolished, the layout being simplified and worked from a console in the cabin at Stainforth until placed under Doncaster's control. The alterations here were accelerated by the construction of a new road bridge which would have affected the visual surveillance of the old manual cabin. Thorne itself has two stations, that at the north side of the town being on the former NE branch to Goole, a substantial affair of quite attractive appearance which has fared better than Thorne South on the old SY route which is now virtually two platforms. This station had some rather dark lodgings beneath it into which returning bucolic excursionists who proved a handful could be pushed. Hooliganism has, indeed, always been a problem and here was one way in which earlier times dealt with it. The presence of facilities at the station must have meant that certain travellers to Cleethorpes for the day must have been in the habit of thorough-going indulgence!

The SY line ran down on the left to the wharf at Keadby. The MS&L built eastwards over the Trent, providing a junction at Gunhouse, or Gunness, a site noteworthy also for its canal bridge carrying the railway which lifted and rolled back on to the approach rails. More famous and spectacular was the nearby Keadby bridge over the Trent, built in 1916 as a replacement for an earlier swing span. The lift span of the newer bridge also carried a roadway and was 160ft. in length. This has now been fixed, as the need for lifting no longer arises. The rail approach was governed by interesting three position semaphore signals which rose to 45 degrees for caution and to vertical for "all clear".

Chapter Four. The Denaby Branch

By 1885 the Hull and Barnsley Railway had already made great efforts and spent not a little money in reaching the northern edge of the South Yorkshire coalfield, running across the level land westwards after surmounting the somewhat daunting barrier of the lower Wolds by means of Drewton tunnel and its attendent cutting of 83 ft. in depth. The company found coal at the extremity of the line, at Wharncliffe Woodmoor and Monckton Main Collieries in the Cudworth area, and also at Upton, a newer mine situated not far from South Elmsall on the main road from Doncaster to Leeds. To Hull, however, the haul was a long one of fifty miles to carry the coal, with a steady pull over the Wolds into the bargain. It was not surprising, therefore, that the H&B decided to look elsewhere within its territory to see what other places might offer in the way of coal. The most obvious place to expand the network was in the young coalfield itself, and so a point was chosen at Wrangbrook, then as now a small hamlet near Upton, from which to run a branch line southwards. Originally this idea was fostered by a separate company as the South Yorkshire Junction Railway of 1894; this concern was virtually the Denaby and Cadeby Colliery Company under a different name. The line was in fact worked by the H&B from the opening day.

From Kirk Smeaton station the H&B ran westwards to pass beneath the A1 trunk road by way of the 1,226 yds. long Barnsdale tunnel, erroneously known at various times as the South Kirkby tunnel. East of this tunnel there existed for a time until the early thirties a small cabin, one of several which the Hull and Barnsley installed in order to split up the long block sections and enable more intensive running to take place. This box was called Barnsdale and, like a similar cabin at Weedley on the run up eastwards to Drewton tunnel, was set in sylvan surroundings and must have been indeed restful and quiet, if a trifle monotonous, to work in.

West of Barnsdale tunnel, once a steep-sided cutting was left behind, an open site was found for Wrangbrook junction, whence the single line branch curved off southwards through fine rolling countryside which demanded cuttings of snug fit alternating with embankments, the former predominating. A sharp dip down a gradient of 1 in 100 brought the line to the brick viaduct with its magnesian limestone toppings which carried it over the main GN and GC Joint line from Doncaster to Leeds. This was at Hampole, a small village once the home of a local legendary hermit, which had a station of wooden construction on the Leeds line until its closure in the fifties. The brick viaduct became somewhat infirm during the 1939-45 war, and spent the last few years of its shored up by baulks of timber. It was replaced by a more prosaic steel girder bridge in about 1960. Either side of the viaduct were two small quarries each having a siding worked by ground frames (Hinchcliffe's and Neville's). From this point the line climbed away at 1 in 100 to arrive on the descending switchback at Pickburn and Brodsworth station, situated at 4 miles 38 chains from Wrangbrook. Here was to be found a passing loop and siding on to the up or west side, where there was also the station approach up from the road leading to Brodsworth, a pretty village about half a mile distant. Pickburn was a hamlet virtually at the station, strung out along the road running parallel to the railway. Soon the rural scene was to be changed, though not too greatly, by the sinking of the Brodsworth colliery on a site east of the line on higher land nearby and quite close to the A1 trunk road. The H&B soon laid down a short branch line having a connection facing south and running into the colliery yard. From the GN and GC Joint line to Leeds, not far distant on the other side of the ridge, and leaving that route by a junction at Castle Hills, a single line of track also came, passing beneath the A1 and through the new colliery village of Woodlands to reach the Brodsworth pit sidings. At Pickburn the installation of the new connection necessitated the building of a newer, larger signal box some yards south of the station.

Running away from Pickburn, the single line went through lovely countryside, the home of fox and hare, past Cusworth Park and encountered a further neat limestone cutting or two before arriving at Sprotborough station, where was to be found a second passing loop and a single siding. The site of the whole lay some little way outside the village to the west within walking distance of the venerable old church and cricket ground visited once a year by the Yorkshire team. Here the line paused before running down a steady 1 in 100 gradient on a ledge, from which the extensive quarries on the other side of the Don Valley at Warmsworth might be glimpsed among the trees of quite a considerable wood. It then passed through a short tunnel and out along yet another ledge which ran intermediately between the Dearne Valley line of the Lancashire and Yorkshire Railway, itself above on its own terrace, and the more comfortably placed GC route below, all three overlooked by the impressive pile of Conisbrough castle and the sturdy viaduct of the Dearne Valley route striding across the Don from Butterbusk. The colliery at Cadeby was sited between GC line and the H&B branch, the former company drawing off coal traffic from siding at Cadeby signal box, the latter from a yard at the end of the line. The extremity of the branch was Denaby, where was situated the colliery of the same name. It was possible to run through on to the GC via the sidings, but some time later, in July 1908, the two companies were linked by a connection running to Lowfield junction which was under the eye of a standard GC pattern cabin. The link involved the construction of a moderately sized girder bridge across the Don.

The most interesting feature of the early working of the line was the slender passenger service which ran from the outset until 1903, there being only two trains each way originating from Denaby and running for some non-apparent reason not merely to Kirk Smeaton, where turntable facilities existed, but an extra ten miles to Carlton, the idea possibly being to connect with the Knottingly service at that station and enhance it as a sort of focal point of the system. The first train left Denaby and Conisbrough at 9.25 a.m., arriving at Carlton at 10.00 a.m. where, after a breather it set off on the return trip at

10.35 a.m. A second run left Denaby at 5 p.m. reaching Carlton at 5.45 p.m., returning from there at 6.20 p.m. At Denaby there was a small wooden shed to house the tank engine; this was later destroyed by fire, the engine continuing to be stabled among the ruins. The station was a wooden affair at the end of a siding controlled by a ground frame. The site was adjacent to the GC line, passengers gaining access thereunder by a subway. In later years the stationmaster's house of standard pattern survived to mark the site. Seven minutes away by passenger train was Sprotborough station, of two platforms on each side of the loop, the principal building being a single-storeyed structure of wood on the north-eastern or down side, together with the ten lever signal box. The up platform was furnished with a jaunty waiting shed. At the turn of the century Mr. Howden was stationmaster of this rather idyllic spot and has some interesting observations to make on life there:

"When stationmaster I remember coming home one evening to find a full-blown cricket match going on in the station, with wickets set up in the six foot way and with the adjacent yard full of spectators. This was after the last train had gone. On my appearance, the match was once 'a draw.' During the first winter I was at Sprotborough station we received a weekly truck load containing approximately five or six tons of corn and so on to feed the pheasants. There were four gamekeepers, and over four hundred pheasants were hatched by hens, in addition to those hatched in the woods. Not infrequently we were disturbed by poachers in the woods stealing the birds." Today the woods have largely gone, along with the line.

Had prizes been awarded in those days for station location and appearance, then Sprotborough would certainly have come high in the league. Having discovered much to admire in the rustic surroundings viewed from the carriage window, the passenger would find himself at Pickburn after a further eight minutes. Here, with the exception of stove pipes for chimneys instead of brick structures, the building was identical to that at Sprotborough, with lapped boarding and the provision of an outside ticket window. A short rest and the train passed out of the scope of this chapter, up the gradient and along the switchback to the parent system at Wrangbrook junction for the run to Kirk Smeaton.

Particularly following the linking of the Denaby branch to the GC at Lowfield junction, the movement of mineral traffic was divided into two sections, with Pickburn as the point of division. Obviously, the GC drew off its traffic from Brodsworth colliery, trains of empties from the south being run round at the station and propelled into the yard, the full loads running out "right away" without any problem. Robinson's eight-coupled locomotives of LNER Class Q4 and 04 worked the southern end of the branch throughout the whole of its, and their, working life. The through link enabled the Mexborough crane to cope with any mishap on the branch, though these were few, the most spectacular being a fall of rock at Skelbrooke into which a loaded mineral train headed by 0-6-0 No. 96 ploughed its way in H&B days in 1907. Trains coming off the H&B main lines seeking coal normally ran to Pickburn for Brodsworth colliery, though some workings would get as far as Denaby and return with whole rakes of loaded wagons, more often then not all in red livery with the same colliery name blazoned on the sides. Normal power was the small 0-6-0 tender locomotive, somewhat puny by Robinson standards—the big H&B 0-8-0s were denied access to the line because of weight limitations, the normal practice being to have an 0-6-2T render banking assistance up the 1 in 100 gradient from Denaby to Sprotborough. No doubt this same tank

A J11 brings a Doncaster Race Week special down the goods lines at Hexthorpe Flatts in September 1950. The coaches are two sets of Gresley quintuplets. *C.T. Goode*

engine would be used to operate the two passenger trips, plus a couple of four-wheelers, to Carlton and back. On occasion a van would be attached.

Due to the terrain, it was not possible at Pickburn to lay in a triangular junction to the colliery yard, which resulted in special working arrangements for trains arriving from the north and vice-versa. Arriving trains were simply run round in the station and propelled into the yard. What transpired with full loads demanded a special note in the Working Appendix:

"In making up full loads of traffic for Wrangbrook, it is necessary to draw half the train, with Brake Van attached next the engine from the loaded sidings to the Colliery Loop Lines, (which hold about thirty five wagons each), where the wagons must be detached. The engine must return to the Loaded Sidings for the remaining half of the train, drawing it on to the same loop as the first portion. The engine then propel the first portion on to the single line towards Pickburn station, return to the rear of the second portion and propel it on to the first portion, when the two portions must be coupled up and the whole train propelled to Pickburn station. A shunter must walk behind each half of these trains when being drawn from the Colliery Loaded Sidings to the Loop Lines and be prepared to apply the hand brakes of any wagons which may from any cause become disconnected from the trains." Pessimism indeed! It is to be hoped that all involved could understand what was required of them.

Trains loads for the GC section were 32 empties from Denaby to Brodsworth, and 30 loaded from Brodsworth to Denaby. H&B crews with their smaller engines were given a harder job, with no apparent restriction on loading and a straight run off up ¾ mile at a curving 1 in 100. However, the Working Appendix does not forget them: "In the event of a freight train being stopped at Pickburn, and after the Driver is in possession of the staff to go forward to Wrangbrook it is necessary to get a better start out of the station, the Driver may be allowed to set back the train a short distance, provided there is nothing in the way." Actually, the worst was yet to come for a loaded train, namely the 1 in 100 up from the viaduct at Hampole going north, and drivers would in fact take advantage of the long similar grade down to that point and trust that their impetus would get them over. Failing that, the usual device of dividing the train and taking half forward would be restored to, this being left in the sidings at Wrangbrook until the second section was recovered.

Wrangbrook became a place of particular importance, especially after the opening of the second branch to Wath in 1902. Here, situated along the two incoming lines, were inter-change sidings, the larger yard being sited west of the Wath branch, and equipped with water-softening plant for the tender supplies and a turntable. Connections at this point were supervised by Wrangbrook West, the East cabin controlling points off the Denaby branch and the main juntion points being under the eye of Wrangbrook North junction. Following a rationalisation programme of about 1934, all the pointwork which remained on the site was brought under the control of Wrangbrook North, now simply "Junction", which became chock full of levers, there being and additional frame of three levers lettered "A, B and C Push and Pull" wedged in at right angles to the main frame by the door.

Mineral traffic off both branches was brought to the sidings at Wrangbrook and re-sorted into acceptable form for forwarding either to Hull or Cudworth, often by a fresh engine. In LNER days, and to the end of branch working, the larger 2-8-0 locomotives did in fact work their trains right through in each direction. As the branch connections faced eastwards, some congestion tended to be caused at the approaches to the junction, itself restricted by a curve in cutting and a looming tunnel mouth, due to trains being reversed for the run to Cudworth. The original three-way junction signal bracket here was most imposing, with tall posts each of the same height. For both the branches a pick-up goods train originated from Cudworth, reversd and called as required at points en route. In LNER days motive power was most likely an ex NE J21 class 0-6-0, though following transfer of power to the Midland depot at Royston on the closure of Cudworth shed in the early fifties more unlikely visitors such as 4Fs and the larger 8Fs were to be encountered on this work.

Mention should be made of the auxiliary token system in operation at Wrangbrook junction for the Denaby branch, whereby a driver was enabled to obtain a token giving him authority to proceed to Pickburn without having to undertake the walk back to the cabin for it. By withdrawing a special key from an instrument in the box, the man at Wrangbrook could insert it into the token instrument, turn it and release one token for the journey. In the early days, too, Wrangbrook also acted as telephone switchboard for messages to and from the branch lines.

Red letter days for operation on the Denaby branch came in May 1952 when the RCTS ran a railtour, headed by B1 No. 61196, which took in the line running northwards. In October 1965 a similar diesel-hauled tour traversed the line in the opposite direction. On one occasion in 1958 on a sunny April morning there could be seen at Pickburn the 8F resting on pick-up duty, a

Hull WD locomotive in the yard and B1 No. 61002 *Impala* waiting on the down line with a director's saloon—a concentration of power indeed! Perhaps the most evocative memory of all, however, was a time in the middle of the last war when a grimy and leaking D20 4-4-0 from Hull, one of the erstwhile NE "racers", was based at Wrangbrook with a couple of equally disreputable clerestory coaches as living quarters for Hull men engaged in carrying out maintenance work in the area.

The end of the Denaby branch as a through route came in the late sixties, the rails and station at Pickburn surviving in the time-honoured abandoned state until about 1968, giving an impression of having succumbed to the brash swathe of motorway roaring alongside which was cut between the station site and the old pit heap. The station was always worth a visit, if only to see the almost untouched array of H&B signals which lasted not quite to the end. Sprotborough fared less happily, the loop going in the thirties and a local quarry constructing a rather vulgar loading ramp wagon top height next to the signal cabin. This ruined the appearance of the down platform, to say nothing of its effect on the attractiveness of the whole. The station building, however, survives as a club house. Down at Denaby what was now to all intents and purposes a spur of the colliery complex ran from Lowfield junction past the now closed Denaby colliery yard beyond Cadeby colliery and just through the tunnel to the Steetley Doloma quarry at milepost ten. The quarry remains, but Denaby and Lowfield junction cabins, Denaby Crossing box and all vestiges of Cadeby and Denaby collieries have completely vanished in a remarkably short time. Wrangbrook has, apart from a rather gaunt line of old railwaymen's cottages, vanished completely without trace, though the main line tunnel still enjoys unofficial use as a useful route for Upton folk visiting the Barnsdale service area on the A1 nearby.

Chapter Five. The Wath Branch

Following on the undoubtedly successful working of the Denaby branch, the Hull and Barnsley embarked on the construction of a second line projected to Wath-on-Dearne, right in the heart of the South Yorkshire coalfield. The line was opened on the last day of March 1902 and was originally double-tracked as far as Hickleton, with a rising gradient favouring loaded coal trains for about the first four miles, then a fall of mainly 1 in 115 to the terminus at Wath. At Wrangbrook junction the line curved away southwards, passing the subsidiary cabin at Wrangbrook West on the down side which controlled a yard on each side of the formation. The down yard on the west side lasted longest and had six roads and a turntable. Adjacent to the road bridge was a water softening plant for the supply to the engines arriving for servicing. A straightish run, gradually rising to cross the main Doncaster to Leeds line (GN & GC Joint), brought the line to Moorhouse and South Elmsall, at 2 miles 31 chains the first station on the branch. Immediately before the station was reached a double line connection came up from the left which had ran from the aforementioned Joint line at Moorhouse junction where a small set of exchange sidings was located. Beyond the station at the neat signal box another connection was thrown off to the west to serve the nearby Frickley colliery which was in fact quite close to the important Swinton and Knottingley Joint line of the North Eastern and Midland companies. This later route ran parellel to the H&B for some distance. Moorhouse station was a smart structure on the up side, away from South Elmsall, a largish centre of population which lay at a futile walk of twenty minutes away. Moorhouse village was in fact on the up side, but was a fair way from the station and only a tiny place of no great passenger potential. The actual building was of red brick and slate, single storeyed with one front gable and a neat glass awning. The gent's outside convenience was of ample proportions fortified by six fire buckets. Platform surfaces were of gravel immaculately kept in the early days, the immediate appearance of the whole being somewhat marred by an impersonal waiting hut on the down side. When approached from the long road out of South Elmsall, the station area on its low embankment looked almost beautiful against the backdrop of the wooded ridge on which could be seen the grey walled village of Hooton Pagnell. From Moorhouse the athletic could walk the undulating three miles or so eastwards and shake hands with the stationmaster at Pickburn on the other branch. At road level on the up side by the underbridge was the stationmaster's house of standard H&B pattern.

Three miles to the south was Hickleton and Thurnscoe station, virtually a copy of that at Moorhouse apart from the platforms which were of wood and having the same yard facilities. The station was one of the few on the Hull and Barnsley system, Howden included, which lay right in the heart of its village, in this case Thurnscoe on a busy road to Barnsley which passed beneath the line north of the site. Thurnscoe with nearby Goldthorpe was quite populous, while Hickleton lay a good ten minutes' walk away up a hill. Immediately south of the station on the down side between the branch and the S&K Joint line was Hickleton colliery, to which both routes had connections and shared a group of sidings. Two signal boxes, one at the station and one at the colliery outlet on the up side, divided the operation of the layout between them, perhaps a somewhat lavish procedure in view of the short distance from one to the other. Just south of the colliery box was what might be termed a near miss for a three level rail crossing with the S&K and the Dearne Valley branch of the Lancashire and Yorkshire company, with a major road thrown in to please the local civil engineer. The latter line ventured a halt at this point, called Goldthorpe after the surrounding village, made up of sleepers and an old coach body. This was however soon reduced to its basic parts by the local lads many years before vandalism became one of the modern art forms. After many years the traffic potential of the S&K through the area has been realised and new halts have been opened at Thurnscoe, adjacent to the old H&B station, but north of the road, and at Goldthorpe in the cutting.

Assuming a somewhat nebulous form the H&B branch now became single and found its way through uninspiring country down the remaining two miles of mainly 1 in 115 to Wath, where it was strategically sited as a terminus between the Midland Railway's main line from Sheffield to Leeds to the north and the Great Central Mexborough to Barnsley route on its southern side. On the single gravel platform face was set a neat building identical to those at the previously mentioned stations. Opposite was a short loading dock and what might be considered an oversized goods shed. The signal cabin stood away from the station on a curve leading to the three road yard, with its short spur for running round, and the private line to Wath colliery. From the main route a spur, virtually double track and of some length, led eastwards to

Manvers Main colliery. The Hull and Barnsley had plans for extending the line from here to Dinnington, some miles to the south-east. At Wath, no turntable seems to have been available. Visually, the greatest impact would be made by the pair of very tall signals governing arriving trains, each on separate posts with subsidiary arms fixed lower down as repeaters because of the intervening Midland overbridge.

A passenger service was operated from the opening day until its withdrawal in April 1929, worked originally by a 2-4-0 and a couple of older coaches. Later the service was operated by a tank engine, sometimes of NE origin. There were some five trains daily between Wath and Kirk Smeaton, plus short workings between Wath and Hickleton which could be served by the same engine. A timetable is shown which gives services in February 1907, together with booked mineral schedules. Passenger trains ran to their own platform face at Kirk Smeaton, where the engine was turned on the turntable on the south side. Mineral engines bound for Wath along the branch were allowed three minutes to detach and turn here before proceeding further— some quiet beefy heaving would be needed to complete that particular manoeuvre in time! Kirk Smeaton was not able to sustain much traffic for main line trains, so it was hardly likely that much would be generated for the branches. It is possible, therefore, that a termination here was simply an operating expedient. Why the Denaby trains never terminated here in the few years prior to the Wath line is something of a mystery, though possibly the island layout at Kirk Smeaton was only put in to coincide with the inauguration of Wath trains.

On the branch itself passenger traffic was healthier, with miners' local trips and a certain amount of excursion traffic, this being maintained into the thirties. On occasions, an excursion would originate at Wath, destination Cleethorpes or Bridlington, picking up at Moorhouse and Hickleton on the way. The route taken would be via the spur at Moorhouse down to the GN & GC Joint line; this later link opened in March 1909 was not normally worked according to the block system, but by telephone. Often the excursions were duplicated, and would return well after midnight to be greeted by augmented station staffs to deal with the livelier and more inebriated characters. It must be remembered that staff on the railway in those days were often expected to work at least twelve hours a day at the rate of about 16s. per week for porters, and for signalmen 21s. to 30s., depending on grade, no overtime being paid for.

Hickleton station had some quite heavy bookings for Doncaster and Barnsley, especially on Saturdays, taxing the available accommodation. Passengers rode to Wath and changed there to the Great Central section, walking the few yards. A porter was posted at the head of the descent to the latter station to shout encouragement to all and sundry, should a train be waiting. Hard by was also the Midland Wath station which could offer facilities for passengers wanting places such as Skipton and Carlisle. Records give little mention of any connections in this direction, however.

Fortunately, a photograph exists of the last passenger train on the Wath branch, pausing at Moorhouse station with an NE tank locomoitve in charge. The regular service survived until April 4th, 1929, being heavily contested by bus interests. Excursion traffic did, however, operate intermittently until the outbreak of hostilities in 1939.

Operation of the coal traffic was quite logical, being drawn from Manvers Main and Wath collieries as available and from Hickleton in competition with the S&K Joint. At Moorhouse, however, the situation was more interesting, since as well as the loads from Frickley colliery to the yard at Wrangbrook, there were also trips to and from the GN and GC Joint line via Moorhouse station, the Hull and Barnsley proper being used for only a short distance between the connecting spurs. In the latter days of working this feature became more and more important at Moorhouse. Theoretically the branch was double tracked to Hickleton, the single line section to Wath falling into virtual disuse after about 1946. On visiting the cabin at Hickleton colliery at that time the author noted the neglect present about the place. He was also shown what appeared to be an old wooden wagon brake scotch used as a baton when required for the section to the terminus, the official block having been discontinued. The branch to the colliery itself was worked by two similar batons, that for the north lines being round and black, the southern one being square and red.

For years the down line from Moorhouse to Wrangbrook was used for the storage of export coal which could not be accepted at the docks in Hull, Wrangbrook yard being too full of loaded wagons. A demand for certain grades of coal caused some interesting shunting problems when it was required to obtain wagons from the centre of the long line. Generally, the motive power was the same in style to that on the Denaby branch, plus the use of the bigger class A 0-8-0s when necessary. There was no shed at Wath.

Sprotborough Station about 1950.   *C.T. Goode*

The passenger locomotive hailed from Cudworth, and the coaches were stored at Kirk Smeaton. Coal workings saw similar motive power to the adjacent branch, with final loads in later years being attended to by Royston 4Fs and 8Fs and Hull WD 2-8-0s.

First to disappear wa the Wath to Hickleton section; then followed that from Hickleton to Moorhouse which was finally worked as a single line. The through branch from Moorhouse into Frickley colliery from the GN and GC line survived for some time but is now no more, with only Moorhouse station house visible. The line to Wrangbrook has gone. Most of the evidence of the existence of the branch has vanished, and in some places like Hickleton its course has been swallowed up by road improvements which have swept away bridge and station. Only at Wath can still be seen a recognisable station building, next to the black and flattened site, called, perhaps not inappropriately, "Barnsley House".

Chapter Six. The South Yorkshire Joint

Two words might aptly sum up the reasons for the sudden onset of activity in the area of the South Yorkshire coalfield in the early years of this century— jealousy and competition. In all, some seven companies were already present in the area in some shape or form, five of them with active lines of their own, and it was perhaps only natural, therefore, that they should each first try to promote schemes of their own to gain a share of the coal now to be produced from the considerable number of pits springing up in the district. Bills were deposited in Parliament for quite an impressive range of schemes, many of which never caused a spade to be lifted in their execution.

The Great Central and Midland companies had already worked together in the Worksop area, where the purely Midland branch from Mansfield via Whitwell reached the GC line from Sheffield to Retford by means of a triangular junction west of Shireoaks, whence a passenger service of Midland trains ran into Worksop's splendid station of assorted waiting rooms and twisted Tudor-style chimneys. It was logical, therefore, that the two concerns should try their luck elsewhere and strike northwards, and so in August 1901 it was proposed that they should construct a route leaving the GC line about one mile west of Shireoaks which would eventually join the GC system not far from Barnby Dun or possibly Conisbrough. This was the Shireoaks, Laughton and Maltby Railway proposal of 1901, of which more later.

The North Eastern and Lancashire and Yorkshire had in mind a line running from Thorne junction to Ravenfield and Dinnington, passing Doncaster on the east side. This would appear to follow in theory the run of the present South Yorkshire Joint line. The Great Northern, ever with a poaching eye, and mindful of the impact it had made by thrusting westwards from Grantham right into the heartland of the Midland at Derby and even beyond that to Stafford, proposed to make a sortie from Bawtry towards Maltby and Rotherham. Both the latter proposal and that of the GC and Midland were to meet up with each other with the construction of Railway No. 11 put forward by the NE which was to leave the Wales (a village near Worksop, not the

Carcroft Station, complete with LNER noticeboards. C.T. Goode

Principality!) and Laughton Light Railway (another non-starter) by a junction running north from a point near the Laughton Common road. It followed the route of what became the South Yorkshire Joint Railway to a point a little beyond the village of Brookhouse, and then ran along a relatively straight course to a point on the Maltby to Blyth road where a trailing junction was to be effected with the suggested Rotherham, Tinsley and Tickhill Railway coming in from the west. Railway No. 11 was to make an end-on junction with the Tickhill Light Railway (see below), and scheduled for the projected route was an impressive viaduct of 117 yds. length to carry the line over Maltby Beck at Roche Abbey.

Other interesting schemes which gave much work and incidental financial benefit to numerous surveyors and draughtsmen might be conveniently mentioned at this point. One such was the Manchester, Midland and Great Grimsby Junction, an idea of the North Midland Railway in which George Hudson had a hand, running from west of Mexborough and passing through the rather sensitive area of Tickhill village. The scheme appears to have foundered here, as with certain modern by-pass suggestions, since it was not established how it would be possible to avoid passing directly through the ruins of Tickhill castle without either burrowing beneath it or knocking it down! A compromise loop to the north was unacceptable to the local farming interests and the idea was abandoned.

The Tickhill Light Railway of 1899 was planned to run from Haxey Junction on the GN and GE Joint line to Lincoln from Doncaster, and thence by way of

(CTD. P. 41)

37

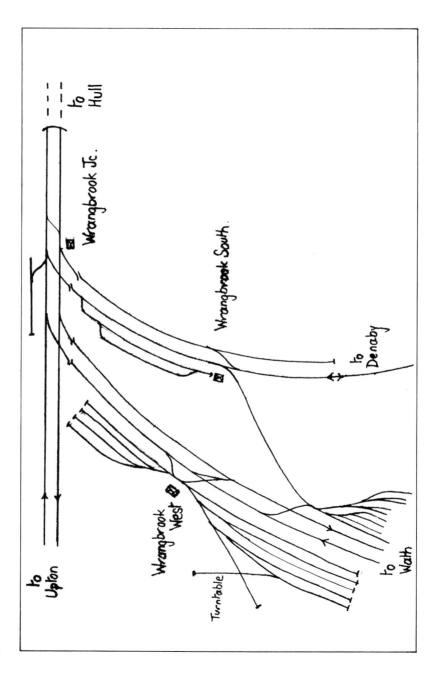

To Hull

Wrangbrook Jc.

Wrangbrook South.

To Denaby

To Upton

Wrangbrook West

Turntable

To Wath

Trains on the Wath Branch February 1907

Down	1	2	4	5	7	8	9
Wath	8.30a.m.	9.40a.m.	11.12a.m.	11.50a.m.	...	1.00p.m.	1.50p.m.
Hickleton Colly.	...	...	...	...	12.45p.m.	...	...
Hickleton	8.38	9.47	11.19	11.58	...	1.07	1.58
Moorhouse	8.45	...	...	12.04p.m.	...	...	2.05
Wrangbrook West	...	...	...	...	...	...	...
Wrangbrook Jc.	...	...	...	...	1.30p.m.	...	...
Kirk Smeaton	8.55	...	...	12.15	...	...	2.15

	11	12	13	14	15	16	17	18
Wath	3.40p.m.	4.45p.m.	6.00p.m.	8.00p.m.	...	8.52p.m.	9.20p.m.	10.15p.m.
Hickleton Colly.	...	...	...	...	8.15p.m.	...	...	...
Hickleton	3.47	4.53	6.17	8.07	8.22	8.59	9.28	...
Moorhouse	...	4.59	6.22	...	...	...	...	...
Wrangbrook West	...	...	...	...	...	...	r	...
Wrangbrook Jc.	...	...	...	...	...	...	...	11.20
Kirk Smeaton	...	5.09	...	...	...	...	9.42	...

Coal trains, Nos. 7, 13, 15 and 18.
Through passenger trains, Nos. 1, 5, 9, 12 and 17.
Miners' passenger trains, Nos. 2, 4, 8, 11 and 14.
No. 15 passed on to the GN at Moorhouse.
The miners' trains are balanced and are worked out and home from Wath, where coaches would have been kept for the purpose.

r—stops on Mons, Weds and Sats as required.

Trains on the Wath Branch February 1907

Up	1	2	3	4	5	6	7
Kirk Smeaton	...	7.30a.m.	9.10a.m.	...	...	...	...
Wrangbrook Jc.	6.47a.m.	...	...	...	...	...	12.30p.m.
Wrangbrook West	7.15	...	...	...	...	11.30a.m.	...
Moorhouse	h	7.40	9.20	...	...	...	...
Hickleton	7.35	7.46	9.26	9.55a.m.	11.25a.m.	11.45	12.40
Hickleton Colly.	8.40	...	...	10.01	11.31	...	12.46
Wath	8.50	7.52	9.32	...	...	...	12.52

Up	8	10	11	12	13	14	15
Kirk Smeaton	...	2.45p.m.	...	...	...	...	...
Wrangbrook Jc.	...	...	...	...	5.28p.m.	...	...
Wrangbrook West	...	...	...	3.52p.m.	...	6.45p.m.	...
Moorhouse	...	3.04	...	4.15	...	...	...
Hickleton	1.20p.m.	3.10	4.21p.m.	h	5.38	...	8.27p.m.
Hickleton Colly.	1.26	...	4.27	4.35	5.44	.705	8.33
Wath	...	3.16	...	5.10	5.50	...	...

Up	16	17	18
Kirk Smeaton	...	...	...
Wrangbrook Jc.	...	...	...
Wrangbrook West	...	...	8.50p.m.
Moorhouse	...	...	...
Hickleton	8.27p.m.	9.05p.m.	9.30
Hickleton Colly.	8.33	9.11	9.40
Wath	...	...	...

Goods and coal empties, Nos. 1, 6, 12, 14 and 18.
Through passenger trains, Nos. 2, 3, 7, 10 and 13.
Miners' passenger trains, Nos. 4, 5, 8, 11, 16 and 17.
h—stops when required.

Bawtry across to Tickhill where a terminal station was originally planned for the main street. This idea was later rejected in favour of a through run faster westwards. In the event this project tended to foreshadow the much later mineral branch from Scrooby GN to Harworth colliery, and also what became a mineral only link between Haxey and Bawtry via Misson. The GN also proposed a scheme for a line to run from Bawtry to the villages of Stainton, Ravenfield and Dinnington, the prime objective at the latter point being the new colliery and coking ovens. This was put forward in 1902 but not developed.

Among other projected lines, two are important as falling into the train of events which actually transpired. One was the proposal of 1901 for a Rotherham, Laughton and Maltby Light Railway, the Order for which was refused twice. This concern had as its chairman Thomas Marrion of Thurcroft Hall, the owner of the rights to the coal in the district. A portion of the proposed line later became part of the South Yorkshire Joint. The second scheme was for an extension of the Hull and Barnsley's Wath branch from a point near Hickleton to Dinnington. This thrust by a very determined company was authorised by an Act of 1902, the line leaving Hickleton colliery box and running south-eastwards parallel to the Dearne Valley line before crossing the Great Central east of Mexborough by a substantial viaduct after having negotiated some difficult terrain. Near the village of Hooton Roberts the route was to describe an "S" bend. A portion of this line was in fact built, namely that from Braithwell to Dinnington, which eventually became the GC, H&B and Midland Joint. This section of line jointly owned by

Hickleton & Thurnscoe Station.   *C.T. Goode*

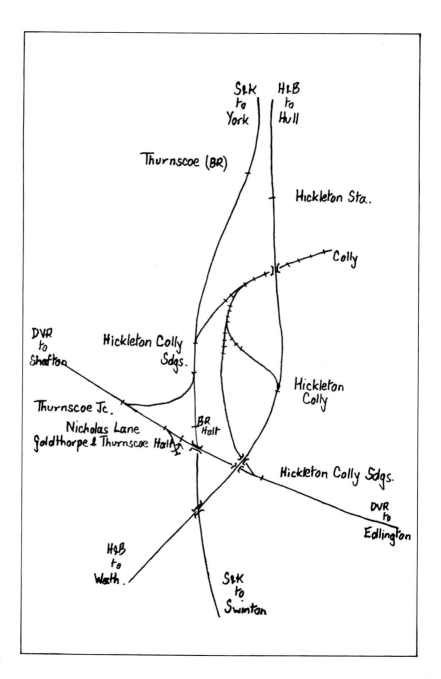

S&K
to
York

H&B
to
Hull

Thurnscoe (BR)

Hickleton Sta.

Colly

DVR
to
Shafton

Hickleton Colly
Sdgs.

Hickleton
Colly

Thurnscoe Jc.

Nicholas Lane
Goldthorpe & Thurnscoe Halt

BR
Halt

Hickleton Colly Sdgs.

DVR
to
Edlington

H&B
to
Wath.

S&K
to
Swinton

the H&B was initially unique in that it remained cut off from the parent concern until 1916 and was only to be reached by working over the GC and Midland Joint (mentioned again below). There is no record of any Hull and Barnsley working over this circuitous route, the GC moving that company's traffic as required.

Of interest was the Rotherham and Bawtry Railway, for which an Act was obtained in 1881, somewhat in advance of other proposals. This line was to leave the Midland direct route from Rotherham to Chesterfield south of the former place and run east to a triangular connection with the GN at Bawtry. The line of route passed close to the final line of the SYJ in the area of Sandbeck and Tickhill and was the first of several proposals which were to plague the Earl of Scarbrough on his considerable estate. The idea was abandoned in 1886.

Had all the various schemes come to fruition, then the map of the borderland of South Yorkshire and North Nottinghamshire would have resembled a veritable fishing net. Fortunately, however, commonsense prevailed and out of the melee came a decision by five of the interested companies to combine in the formation of a purposeful joint line running from north to south through the coalfield near to its eastern border. Prime movers in the establishment of the concern were the Midland and Great Central, who persuaded the North Eastern and the Lancashire and Yorkshire companies to adopt what became the final line of route. The Great Northern, which had been instrumental in promoting schemes of its own, reluctantly abandoned them and fell in with the majority. It is interesting to note at this stage that, in due course, it was the GN and GC who were most readily in evidence on the operating side. In February 1903 the first reading of the Joint Line Bill was heard in Parliament and was passed later in the same year.

Before the South Yorkshire Joint Railway is built, as it were, it is essential to set down and select from the vague projects already mentioned those other lines at the southern end with which it was connected. The GC and Midland joint venture with ambitions taking it from Shireoaks to Barnby Dun did in fact produce a more modest line which began as planned one mile west of Shireoaks at Brancliffe junction and ran north-westwards for 3½ miles to Dinnington colliery, just north of Anston junction. This section was opened in October 1905. From Anston junction the new line ran north, leaving the Dinnington colliery on a spur to the east and making an end-on connection with the GC, H&B and Midland Joint, which had Thurcroft colliery on its route. At Braithwell junction the GC and H&B went jointly to the north to make eventual union with the latter company's main line at Aire junction, though this was not to be until 1916. The westerly fork at Braithwell was opened by the GC and Midland and ran by way of Silverwood colliery to Thrybergh junction and Roundwood junction, on each of the parent systems respectively, this piece of line getting its first airing in 1905 and embodying a private concern of 1901 running coal down from Silverwood colliery (Dalton) to the main lines. It will thus be realised that railway activity was quite complicated enough in the area, even with joint efforts. Behind all these fusions lay the Great Central, quietly empire-building.

Construction of the South Yorkshire Joint Line was handed to a Leeds firm, Whittaker Bros., and was begun in the vicinity of the Dinnington colliery sidings by the Rotherham Road bridge in November 1905. From here the double track passed northwards through Dinnington station, the first of three similarly built red brick structures, the principal offices being east of the line and served by a moderately sized goods yard. Double track was extended to Dinnington North box in 1913, several yards beyond the station, and from here made its way in a generally northerly direction by falling gradients of between 1 in 113 and 1 in 150 to Maltby station at a little short of nine miles from Brancliffe junction. Close to the two small villages of Brookhouse and Slade Hooton, the latter well-placed for a halt, the line passed over a small stream in a largish valley by means of a skew lattice viaduct of five spans. Three hundred tons of steel were used in its construction and only accommodation for a single line was completed, though the brick abutments left room for doubling on the south-east side. The maximum height of the structure above the road below was 40ft. The terrain dictated further engineering work beyond this point in the shape of two deep cuttings—one of ¾ mile in length and 35ft. deep, the other of ½ mile and of 57ft. depth—through magnesian limestone which, in its crushed state, was useful for finishing the line. An early draft plan for the construction of the line reveals a much more ambitious scheme of building which produced gradients of 1 in 156, 288 and a lengthy 1 in 533 up to a tunnel of no less than 1,980 yds. with a maximum depth of 75ft. some 4½ miles from the Laughton Common road, the line falling at a maximum of 1 in 105 to 9 miles 7 furlongs at the junction with the nebulous Tickhill Light Railway. On this stretch, as well as the tunnel, were to be included 12 bridges and a viaduct.

Work on the line progressed very smoothly with the use of several steam excavators loading the spoil into some 400 tipper wagons marshalled by the contractor's 14 locomotives. On a falling gradient of 1 in 113 the line entered Maltby station, a little under halfway. Here the building was identical to that at Dinnington, the principal block being on the north side adjacent to the yard, linked to the other platform by a lattice girder bridge for pedestrians. The cost of the buildings, performed by Salmon of Cudworth, came to £4,738. Maltby Colliery, controlled by the Sheepbridge Iron and Coal Company, was begun in 1908 and became operational in 1910. Dinnington Colliery, worked beneath land owned by the Earl of Scarbrough, had reached the Barnsley seam earlier, in 1904. Three signal boxes ultimately served the Maltby area, all on the east side of the line, there being one controlling the goods yard, and then to the north a larger signal cabin serving the colliery yard. Due to traffic improvements a further cabin was erected some half a mile to the north in December 1913, these two being known as Maltby Colliery North and South respectively. Double track passed through this quite busy site, still very active today.

From the Maltby colliery yard the single line ran north into fairly difficult terrain, entering a cutting of moderate depth and describing an "S" bend, turning east and then north again by the village of Stainton, the birthplace of the famous cricketer Freddie Trueman. Shortly after this point, by steadily falling gradients, the triangular layout of Firbeck junction was reached at two miles from Maltby station. This layout did not feature in the original conception of the SYJ, but was in fact to become virtually the heart of the system in its final form. An Act was obtained in 1914 for a branch to Harworth, where a new colliery was in fact opened in 1929. A Light Railway Order of 1916 was then obtained for a branch to another new mine at Firbeck, but setbacks due to the war caused the branch from Firbeck junction and the line of 1916 to Firbeck colliery to be opened only in 1927, a considerable delay in the realisation of the idea. The SYJ Committee had initially been spurred on to take traffic from the colliery workings by their owners, the Sheepbridge Co., who had applied for an Act to construct a line from Worksop to Bawtry by way of Firbeck and Harworth. Competition was also on hand from the GN which was able to draw off Harworth coal by means of short branch from their own main line at Scrooby. Ultimately the two branches were to meet at Harworth colliery, in the yard of which trains could pass from one branch on to the other.

Although, therefore a post-Grouping adjunct to the SYJ, the triangle at Firbeck held much of the atmosphere of the line with a full set of vintage GC signals and two of that company's standard cabins. Firbeck "A" dealt with the main line and connections to the east in the direction of the collieries, where Firbeck "B" was positioned at that point of the triangle. The cabin here did in fact come from elsewhere on the SYJ—Grange, at the northern end, which the LNER converted to spring point operation. Beyond Firbeck "B" the single line divided into two at Harworth junction, running to that colliery and to Firbeck respectively. All three junctions of the triangle at Firbeck were double tracked within the points, the single line proceeding beyond in each of the three directions. The area was fully track-circuited as all the approaches were curved and in cutting. Several interesting features were embodied in the layout here, one being the provision of extra signalling—brought into use when required by a king lever— in order that the down line (to Tickhill) might be used for two way working when the cabin was closed. In the event it seems that this facility was rarely used—indeed, Tickhill station was more often switched out and the equipment was soon removed. When in section, the single lines were controlled by the key token system and, as the original run between Maltby and Tickhill was worked by Tyers No. 6 tablet instruments which were linked together when Firbeck was switched out, this made for a somewhat complicated switching arrangement inter-related with the mechanical locking when closure took place. At Firbeck were also auxiliary key token instruments. Due to the central position of Firbeck "A" cabin within the triangular layout, subsidiary token instruments were provided at Firbeck "B" to render and accommodate tokens offered by trains going round the north and south curves to the collieries from either Maltby or Tickhill, thus saving the crews a considerable walk to the "A" cabin. Possibly this would be the only way of coping with a situation of this nature on a single track, though an alternative might well have been to permit both Tickhill and Maltby to issue tokens direct to Firbeck "B".

Tickhill station, at 3¾ miles from Maltby and 12½ miles from Brancliffe junction, had a passing loop, though eventually the traffic proved to be light in the thirties and a similar system to that at Firbeck was instituted whereby trains could pass along the down line in both directions when the cabin was closed, a king lever bringing in the necessary signalling. Due to its strategic position Firbeck was always open during running and itself needed two sets of single line instruments at the north end—one for tokens to work to and from Tickhill, the other for the tablets to St. Catherine's junction when Tickhill was "out". The station at Tickhill was identical with the other two, the main offices and yard with crane being on the up or Tickhill side, and the village being a solid twenty minutes' walk away. The two platforms were linked by the standard lattice footbridge, a luxury at all three stations as the available road bridge could well have been utilised as was the case with other companies. The station was named Tickhill and Wadworth in 1911, the latter village lying also a twenty minute trek away. Apparently this was the second site for the station, the earlier being most likely on the Stainton road where it crossed the line near the Firbeck triangle. In any event either would be in an unpopular position for easy access. No industry was ever adjacent to the line here, and the site enjoyed a delightfully rustic atmosphere.

The line of route proceeded by way of falling gradients to the plain area known as the Carrs, south-east of Doncaster, the haunt of marsh life and duck shooters. At 15¼ miles from Brancliffe junction, and almost three miles from Tickhill was St. Catherine's junction, one of the most remote cabins in the area, even though within sight of Doncaster's chimneys. Signalmen must leave their vehicles quite a way down the lane and reach the box after ten minute walk. St. Catherine's, originally Potteric Carr, its present name hailing from either the nearby hospital or Loversall church across the fields, had a theoretical 50 levers and was the largest on the SYJ. Had all the connections envisaged at this point materialised, then all 50 would have been used as the cabin lay at the southern edge of a most impressive filigree of lines over which the Joint line moved majestically by two lowish lattice viaducts, the longer spanning the GN prime route to King's Cross from Doncaster which chose this location to send off its own Joint line with the Great Eastern to Lincoln and East Anglia. In fact, the latter was the original route from south to north. The other line encountered was the Dearne Valley branch of the Lancashire and Yorkshire company, itself a single line joining the GN and GE Joint line at Bessacarr junction and also the GN proper at Loversall Carr junction, connections being made by a unique and impressive system of flying junctions. The Dearne Valley also spawned a range of storage sidings beneath the SYJ viaduct. At St. Catherine's, from the formation which became double track, an up and down spur ran west to the Dearne Valley line which was opened by that company in 1908. Next a spur, also of double line, ran eastwards to the Dearne Valley, this being L&Y, GN and NE Joint owned of 1909-10. As if this were not enough, a further single line ran north-west by a viaduct of its own round to the down side of the GN main line at Childers Drain. This line was evidently not taken seriously, for it connected with the GN sidings and ran into the SYJ by a trailing connection with the up line only. Full scale connection with the GN occurred once the SYJ had crossed it, as a sweeping arc of double track led down from the small cabin at Low Ellers junction to Potteric Carr junction (GN). The down connection of this spur fed into the GN down main, the corresponding up line leaving the up slow. This link was probably the most vital lifeline of the Joint company, certainly for the passenger trains, all of which passed this way.

From Low Ellers junction the line became single again and purely mineral in character, the passenger service having been left behind to join the GN. In a short time it passed under the main A1 road near Cantley Lane end, at which point was situated a water tank to replenish the supplies of locomotives in need. The tank was on the down side, but as the line was single the facility was available for trains in both directions. At its base was a type of letter box into which enginemen had to deposit a form, there being one each for "tender of water" or "tank of water" as might fit the particular case. Supplies of water were metered from Doncaster Corporation. A working timetable for 1913 gives no less than four trains stopping for water in the down direction, these all being NE workings ex Dinnington colliery for Hull. NE tenders were often small, the run was a long one and no doubt the refreshment was greatly appreciated.

The route passed north-eastwards round the Doncaster racecourse which had in no way to be crossed or truncated in the course of the line's construction. Nearby, however, lay the shooting butts of the Doncaster Rifle

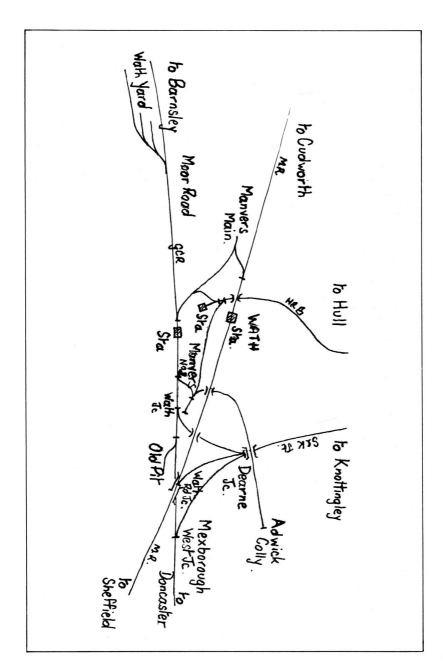

47

The hub of the H&B in South Yorkshire, Wrangbrook Jc. looking east in
1948.   *C.T. Goode*

Club which, being originally across the route of the railway, had to be resited
in 1904 to one side of what became the airfield. In 1904-5 the company toyed
with the idea of erecting a platform by the racecourse to cope with the
lucrative tidal traffic of punters; this, to be called Cantley, would most likely
have been a profitable investment in the days when every lettable room in
Doncaster was pressed into service during St. Leger week to satisfy the
throng of pleasure-seeking gentry and all other classes. A loading dock for
horses could have been introduced without any fuss whatever, and would
have saved both punters and horses a lengthy trek from the town's principal
station. These happy ideas were swiftly scotched by the GN which felt that it
was already doing a fine job in this direction.

In Sandall Beat Woods was Markham Sidings signal box, a relative
youngster on the system, installed in 1926 at the time when the Markham
colliery was opened with an output exclusive to the SYJ. It was served by a
run of sidings on the up, or east side, and a long passing loop. The cabin and
its attendant signalling, though late on the scene, was vintage GC and
boasted no track circuiting, although the signalman was at a marked
disadvantage, badly placed on the inside of the curve. There was, however, a
device placed on the single line approach at the northern end out of sight
called a treadle annunciator, an interesting name for a form of fouling bar
which, when depressed by an oncoming train, rings a bell in the cabin.
Woodland surrounds the site here which is virtually level and in some ways
remote. It is recorded that a goods depot was provided at Markham in 1918,

48

though lineside observations do not readily reveal the original whereabouts of this—possibly it was up by the road bridge. Certainly the site was known as Armthorpe (after the nearest village) during the early years of the line. The Markham sidings site in its final form is distinguished only by a long footbridge which takes a path into the colliery yard.

After crossing the main A18 road from Doncaster to Hatfield the line becomes double at Grange spring points, 20 miles from Brancliffe junction, preparatory to running into the GC four-track route from Doncaster to Cleethorpes at Kirk Sandall junction, where the usual connections were made with all four lines, both slow and fast in each direction. Between Kirk Sandall junction and Low Ellers the key token system was in use. The original Kirk Sandall cabin was situated at 2 miles 279 yds. from Bentley junction (the nearer block post to Doncaster) in the fork of the intersection. On the quadrupling of the GC route in 1916 the typically Gorton-inspired cabin was constructed on the east side at 2 miles 510 yds. controlling extensive works' connections to premises across the running lines. The original cabin at Grange was closed about 1925, its humble functions once carried out by signalwomen being replaced by spring points. The cabin was not lost however, and as already noted went to become Firbeck "B", thus keeping it in the family.

Chapter Seven. Trials and Tribulations of SYJ Operations

With five companies moving coal to and from along its length, the South Yorkshire Joint Railway, which it must be remembered possessed neither locomotives nor rolling stock of its own, presented quite an interesting spectacle for much of its existence and the individual constituents were readily advertised almost up to nationalisation by their distinctive locomotives. Keenest at the outset was the Lancashire and Yorkshire which was soon off the mark in 1909, moving coal from Dinnington northwards behind its somewhat austere looking but powerful 0-8-0 goods engines to St. Catherine's and thence to the Dearne Valley route. A high-handed attitude over a working agreement with the Great Central terminating the use of lines owned by the L&Y in the area of Ancoats junction, Manchester, by GC trains of coal, soon caused a rift in the lute and made the two concerns uneasy bedfellows for many years. Most of the coal produced was exported, running to Grimsby in GC trains and to Hull by the North Eastern. Partly to meet this new flow of traffic the GC line from Doncaster to Thorne junction was quadrupled in 1916, there being the sizeable colliery at Hatfield Main also en route. GC traffic entered and left the line chiefly from the southern end at Brancliffe junction, the eastwards facing connection favouring trains bound for Grimsby via Retford, where was situated the notorious flat crossing with the main GN route. The GC produced its own 0-8-0 tender engine, a more mellow looking machine than that of the L&Y with an interesting set of curved splashers over its wheels which were set close together to give a "ready to pounce" look. Later of course, and indeed right to the end of steam, the Robinson 2-8-0s were seen daily.

The Midland company put in an appearance at Dinnington colliery three times a day, returning to its own metals via Shireoaks and Woodend. In the pre-1914 period the company seems to have handled the morning pick-up goods service at the stations to Tickhill, the working reaching there at 12.53 p.m. and remaining just long enough for a sandwich. The Midland never had an 0-8-0 to flaunt in the faces of the others, so perhaps one of the ubiquitous 3F 0-6-0s would be used for the turn, possibly from Kirkby-in-Ashfield shed. It would be interesting to know by what guile the Midland secured this working; certainly it was the GC which operated the afternoon pick-up, most probably with a Retford "Pompom" 0-6-0, though that concern had a way of pressing the most unlikely motive power into service on menial tasks—even a "Sir Sam Fay" would have raised no eyebrows on the turn. The North Eastern worked its coal traffic with three or four trains off the northern end of the line, employing one of three types of 0-8-0 locomotive, including the powerful Q6 design. The trains were grateful for the provision of watering facilities at Cantley bridge, supplies being taken on the home run. The GN had a share with the GC in the passenger operation and also, because it was perhaps convenient, supplied breakdown facilities if needed. It only had a single booked mineral working on and off the branch, which is perhaps surprising. Again, a "Long Tom" 0-8-0 would be used, or perhaps one of the multifarious 0-6-0s which were often asthmatic and underpowered. Trains of locomotive coal would be collected casually by the GN as required, loads of up to 45 wagons being propelled to and from St. Catherine's junction. If this number were exceeded, then two brake vans were provided and the train run round. On one memorable evening a small GN engine took 42 wagons of coal from Markham to Kirk Sandall to become stuck on the 1 in 200 halfway between the two places. In extremely cold weather the time was spent in dividing, running forward with twenty-eight vehicles and then returning for the rest.

There was, then, quite a kaleidoscope of motive power with a modest basis of thirteen booked mineral and pick-up workings in the early days. By 1970 this had grown somewhat to around 20 runs, mainly serving power stations, the export coal having largely disappeared. What has gone, of course, with the steam engines and indeed long before them are the long rakes of private owner wagons, mostly in red with their white lettering denoting particular ownership. Here and there one would gain an unexpected bonus in a yellow wagon (Spiers) or blue (Dearne Valley Colliery) or a beautifully handwritten name full of poetry, such as "Hannah Samwell".

The Great War took several of the staff away to fight for their country, though fortunately without many casualties. A certain amount of military goods traffic was handled in the area, as at Tickhill. Some documents of the period shed some light on this:-

27th March, 1916: GN Military Special stuck in section between Tickhill and Maltby. Left Tickhill at 8.27 a.m. Cleared at 9.48 a.m. 9.07 a.m. passenger delayed nineteen minutes.

13th March, 1916: Mr. W. Root loaded 60 tons of hay at Tickhill.

8th April, 1916: Six wagons, eight sheets required for Military Hay Traffic.

26th April, 1916: Portable engine sent to Filey from Tickhill. Weight 7½ tons. 9 feet high, 18 feet long, width 4 feet 7 inches. Also hay pressing machine 20 feet long, 8 feet high and 6 feet 8 inches wide.

Relief telegrams of the post Great War period lend a little colour to the traffic movements; they were sent from Tickhill:-

7th December, 1920: GN engine No. 606. Driver B. Bean. Relief requested.

16th December, 1920: To Controller Worksop. GC engine No. 790 (0-6-0) on 3.30 p.m. ex Armthorpe to Worksop. Requesting relief. Sent at 6.30 p.m. after what must have been a slow crawl!

20th December, 1920: GN engine No. 1124. Driver A. Theakstone. Relief requested at 5.05 p.m.

Seen occasionally in a mineral train, usually being hustled round the curve to the GN at Potteric Carr next to a GC 0-8-0, would be a van containing traffic including clean laundry which had been loaded at Maltby from Lord Scarbrough's estate at Sandbeck, its destination being His Lordship's town house in London. At Doncaster the engine would take the van across to the up side, where it would be attached to a southbound parcels train.

Passenger services were very slender throughout their operation and it was quite clear at the outset that the Committee was not particularly interested in introducing them. In April and May 1909 some encouragement was given by various locally interested bodies such as the Worksop Urban District Council, but it was not until 20th June, 1910, that the first two trains—once a miners' excursion from Dinnington to Doncaster in connection with a Rally, the other a well-filled Sunday school trip from Dinnington to Cleethorpes—ran as a foretaste of things which might come. In spite of the popularity of these and of the excursions, plus the steady stream of requests from various parties private and public for a service, it was not until 1st December, 1910, that a regular timetable materialised, subject to certain conditions, one being that no more than four trains a day should be run within a maximum operating period of the signal boxes of twelve hours. To house the first class passengers, composite coaches were to be provided, this stipulation being partially responsible for the non-appearance of any rail motor such as had been seen on many other comparable lines. The GC did in fact run a composite rail motor on the Barton to New Holland branch in North Lincolnshire. Originally, trains were to run between Doncaster and Worksop on a 54 minute schedule, the earliest leaving Worksop at 8.20a.m. and the latest run out of Doncaster being at 5.30p.m., within the twelve hour limit. This created difficulties for commuters into Doncaster who could not reach work in time; neither could schoolchildren. Farmers found the services useless for attending market. As a token gesture therefore the first run was advanced to leave Shireoaks at 7.47a.m. giving an earlier arrival in Doncaster. Little else was in fact done to suit passengers, though a late train was tried for a short time, foundering on the plaguing factor of the overtime bill incurred for the signalmen. Already, in 1911, it was realised that the passenger services were losing money, hardly surprising in view of the rigorous timetable, and the running was reduced to three round trips daily, operated by a Mexborough C13 4-4-2 tank engine. Services ran to Shireoaks only, and rental for the use of Doncaster station was reduced. Every penny counted.

Coal strikes affected the future of the line prior to the Great War, and the revenue returns looked gloomy until the calm before the storm of 1913 with the development of mines in the area. Traffic improved all round, signal boxes opened for most of the day and extra workers' trains were put on from Doncaster to offer transport to a new generation of miners—this in competition with a young and lively bus concern in the Maltby, Dinnington and Tickhill areas. During 1913 some 200 passengers per day were carried on average, bringing in £3,046; not a princely sum, and not able to ring the bells with a profit, but nevertheless providing what must have been a well-needed fillip for the line.

Dinnington, with a staff of fifteen, was the most vigorous station on the line. Its catchment area covered the major colliery village of about 7,000 people, plus Laughton and nearby Thurcroft, all these places being wooed by road transport operators. Lukewarm interest in passengers by the Committee, plus a badly placed station site, must have acted against the promotion of any large scale station usage. Many must have been put off using the train when faced with a two mile walk from the centre of Dinnington to the windy spot on Laughton Common. In fairness, however, it must be said that to position the station nearer the village would have created greater financial and engineering problems. Today one platform exists at Dinnington, possibly against the outside chance of a yearly miners' excursion ever materialising again. The line is single through the site and only the Colliery Junction cabin is open. Most folk here travel to Rotherham and Sheffield for shopping and entertainment. The old rival to the railway, the East Midland bus service to Doncaster, takes over the one hour en route, much longer than the train ever did.

Tickhill and Wadworth station fell enquidistant between the two villages, again inconvenient though with the benefit of local horse-drawn transport for those who did not choose to add walking to their outings. Mr. W. Briggs, who became superintendent, was the first stationmaster here, followed by Mr. C. England who held the office for thirty years until retirement in 1950. With the station master at Tickhill were seven other staff who had no colliery about which to worry, the only fuel being that handled by merchants using the yard. In the yard was the only crane on the line, a five tonner. Passenger traffic was fairly light and again suffered from the nagging local bus service which passed through the heart of the places it served. Here, too, only the down platform has been left after the removal of the passing loop, though the disintegrating station building and siding access to a scrap dealer's on the up side by means of a ground frame still remain.

Maltby station fared more or less the same as the other places. It was also sited well outside the village and, as mentioned previously, might well have enjoyed a more advantageous position if other schemes had come to fruition. People were prepared to use the service, however, and at times in the twenties the trains were well filled. The station was also well placed for the nearby colliery. Rotherham Corporation provided keen competition, and the forerunners of the present East Midland company ran buses to Doncaster and Worksop. Today, the buildings just survive on the down side, with the single line passing through. A platform has been left, possibly with excursion traffic in mind.

During the Great War the passenger service was reduced to Saturdays only after the dark days of 1917. This state of things persisted until 8th November, 1920, when the daily programme was resumed, running to Worksop beyond Shireoaks with two out and back trains to Doncaster from that station. A coal dispute in 1921 led to further demands for the discontinuation of the service by the Committee without success except for the withdrawal of a late Saturday train which, it was said, cost £900 per annum in extra signalmen's hours to run. Extra excursions run for miners and their families were popular, though to some extent revenue from these depended on full employment and the Clerk of the Weather. Race week at Doncaster also provided some heartening booking office returns. On 9th September, 1920, 84 passengers joined the 8.16 a.m. train to Doncaster at Tickhill, whereas on a normal day at the station during the same period the following is typical:-

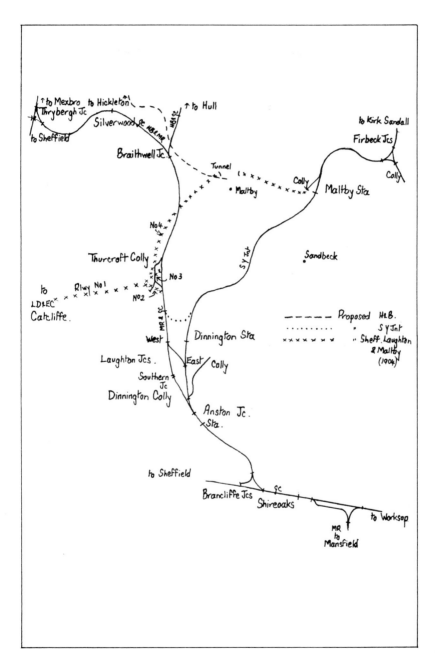

53

Tickets sold for the trains indicated, and cash taken.

  8.16 a.m.   4 singles. 3s. 6d.
  9.22 a.m.   2 returns. 9s.
12.01 p.m.   8 singles. 10 returns. £1.0s. 7½d.
  2.10 p.m.   Nil.
  4.21 p.m.   4 singles. 3s. 6d.
  5.30 p.m.   (Special) Nil.
  6.07 p.m.   Nil.

Total passenger receipts for the day £1-16s-7½d.

However, the 6.07 p.m. did bring a can of film for the Tickhill Picture Palace, so perhaps the halt was justified!

The unloved and unsung passenger train ran its last on 2nd December, 1929, after being withdrawn during 1926-7 as a result of the Coal Strike. In 1928 one of the new 'Sentinel' steam railcars was given trials over the line, though only Third Class accommodation would be available. Excursion traffic continued during the thirties and the trains were usually well patronised. In 1930 the excursions carried passengers to the number of about 9,000, similar to the previous year when the regular service ran. During 1934-6 some 34,000 passengers were carried by the occasional trains, though within this period some regular trains were run on Saturdays between Doncaster, Maltby and Worksop as an experiment without, however, much financial success. Without doubt the excursion traffic kept the station buildings in good order for much longer than would have been the case.

Today the SYJ remains very much alive as a coal carrying line with quite intensive activity at times in the yard at Maltby which retains one of its North and South cabins. Traffic from here runs off in both directions, chiefly to power stations. Dinnington colliery has, along with Thurcroft at the end of what is now a single line remainder of the former GC, H&B and Midland Joint, a reasonable output which is taken southwards via Brancliffe junction. Harworth colliery suffered a reduction in output, as a result of which the GN branch from Scrooby closed in 1965. Thus, that colliery's production is handled solely by the SYJ through Firbeck junction. Firbeck Colliery closed in 1968, taking the branch with it. In 1970 estimated coal tonnage moved on the lines in question was over 1¾ million, no trifling amount. Markham Main has a brisk output worked north to the former GC. At Kirk Sandall junction a connection has been laid in to serve a new factory, quite an event in these days of recession. Rationalisation has taken away all the individual signal cabins in the area of the Carrs.

Two interesting excursions have run over the line in recent years, one being the RCTS railtour of May 1952 which ran southwards, the B1 4-6-0 No. 61195 being unfortunately tender-first for the whole run. The other was the Gainsborough Model Railway Society's run of 12th October, 1963, taking the route northwards, passing Brancliffe junction at 2.25p.m., reaching Maltby at 2.58p.m. for a ten minute breather and passing Tickhill at 3.24p.m. It was perhaps fitting that the train was hauled by a Robinson 2-8-0 of Class 04 in original condition, one of many which had performed so reliably on the line.

||||| *HOW DODWORTH FITS IN*

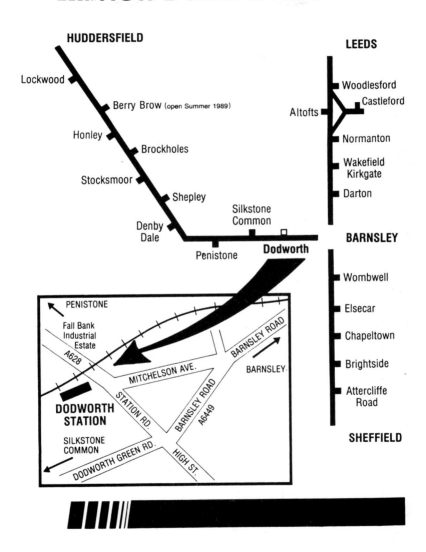

HUDDERSFIELD

Lockwood

Berry Brow (open Summer 1989)

Honley

Brockholes

Stocksmoor

Shepley

Denby
Dale

Penistone

Silkstone
Common

Dodworth

LEEDS

Woodlesford

Castleford

Altofts

Normanton

Wakefield
Kirkgate

Darton

BARNSLEY

Wombwell

Elsecar

Chapeltown

Brightside

Attercliffe
Road

SHEFFIELD

PENISTONE

Fall Bank
Industrial
Estate

A628

MITCHELSON AVE.

BARNSLEY ROAD

BARNSLEY

**DODWORTH
STATION**

STATION RD.

BARNSLEY ROAD
A6449

SILKSTONE
COMMON

DODWORTH GREEN RD.

HIGH ST.

Chapter Eight. The Hull & Barnsley and Great Central Joint

The most remarkable thing about the Hull and Barnsley and Great Central Joint line is that it was ever built at all, its purpose being the rather tenuous one of conveying coal from four collieries, each already provided with an alternative rail outlet, to the Hull and Barnsley system over its 21 rural miles. Stations, of which there were five, were planned with possible residential development in mind; possibly due to the Great War and the insidious spread of road competiiton this aspect of the business was not proceeded with. In 1909 the H&B and GC secured an Act to promote the line, the latter company gaining a third share. The H&B was rather keen on the Midland—with which it was cheek by jowl at the Cudworth end of its system and with which it enjoyed successful working agreements—having a good share of running powers over the line, and also admitting the North Eastern for some strange reason, possibly financial. The H&B and the NE were of course at daggers drawn for all their separate lives. The GC sensed this manoeuvring and advanced its interest to one half, officially endorsed by the GC Act of 1910. North Eastern, Midland and Lancashire and Yorkshire trains could use the line if they wished; also the Great Northern which exercised its right over the short section to Yorkshire Main Colliery from Hexthorpe juncton. Thus, the Hull and Barnsley and Great Central Joint Committee was born.

Construction went ahead at a pace as leisurely as the later operation, the line being begun by Logan and Hemingway in 1911 but not completed and opened throughout until 1st May, 1916. Some confusion has always existed as to exactly where the route left the parent system of the H&B—not surprising as it was in inaccessible though flat countryside and ran across fields on a high embankment. Near the tiny village of Gowdall were two signal boxes, both controlling junctions, the easterly one known as Aire junction situated by the river which is crossed by a bow-string girder bridge and where the Joint line ran away as a double track southwards. Only 1,036 yds. west of Aire junction was Gowdall junction, the point of departure for a spur down to the L&Y line Goole to Knottingley. This spur is still in use, along with a stretch of the H&B through the site of Carlton Towers station to the power station at Drax.

As the countryside is predominantly flat, gradients as far as Doncaster were no great problem for the contractors, apart from places where the formation rose and fell to clear other lines or rivers. From Aire junction the first point of interest was Snaith and Pollington station at 1 mile 1,015 yds., placed south of a level crossing with the main road from Goole to Knottingley. The M62 motorway passes through the site. Here, as well as at the crossing, the signal box of H&B pattern with criss-cross handrails controlled a reasonable sized goods yard of four roads on the down (west) side together with a headshunt. The platforms were constructed of brick with gravel surfaces. Only the foundations of the station buildings appeared on the up side, though a weighbridge and a loading dock were provided. At the crossing a substantial stationmaster's house of rather advanced 1930s "desirable villa" pattern was built of brick and grey pebbledash facing. A similar house was to be found at each location on the Joint line.

The layout at Sykehouse station, 2 miles 606 yds. further south, was similar to that at Snaith with a level crossing and main buildings in an incomplete state on the up side with loading dock and weigh office. Between the two stations mentioned was a Scherzer rolling lift bridge over the Aire and Calder canal built by the Stanningley Iron Works of Leeds. "Scherzer" means "joker" in German, and the term is perhaps not inappropriate for the bridge looked impressive enough until one studied it carefully and found that the whole of the lifting span was fixed and had no engine or gearing to operate it!

Some 4½ miles south of Sykehouse through plain but fertile countryside Thorpe-in-Balne station was reached, the line passing beneath its first overbridge. The station here was sited on a curve and was destined to be of wood, possibly due to the marshy nature of the land. Wooden platforms were laid and the beginnings of a wooden buildings could be seen on both sides— at one place a gate was erected without a fence on either side of it. The signal cabin, which was nearly always closed as it had no active level crossing to attend to, lay out of sight on the down side. The yard here had only two roads situated across the line from the cabin and was provided with the standard weigh office.

Turning south-westwards the line traversed flat land criss-crossed by drains and streams and then rose to cross first the West Riding and Grimsby Joint line of the GN and GC above Applehurst junction, and then the GN main line, before running south to what might be termed its first objective, Bullcroft junction at 2 miles 230 yds. With 57 levers, an odd number of which 37 were used, the box was the largest on the line and controlled a short double spur running east to Bentley colliery, also served by the GN off the main line, and a longer run of single track running west to Bullcroft colliery. This last met the aforementioned West Riding and Grimsby line at Skellow junction, near the colliery yard, arriving by means of a rather noteworthy flying junction. Off the Bentley line was situated a small locomotive depot which housed the H&B shunting pilot. Sidings here were in two groups, both on the down side, "A" being of three roads and "B", which faced north for loaded trains, of six roads.

No station was provided at Bullcroft junction, nor was any provision made for miners' specials. In many ways Bullcroft was the demarcation point between the Hull and Barnsley and Great Central spheres of operation, and as one proceeded south past Bentley pit heap and drab surroundings, the transformation gradually took place. The route passed over the GN again, this time climbing over the line from Doncaster to Leeds and then made a distinct sweep round to the south-east to reach the triangular layout at Doncaster junction (2 miles 993 yds). Here, a signal box of 36 levers was set roughly in the centre of a triangular layout on the up side, the spur off the triangle running half a mile or so to a terminus at Doncaster York Road situated as near as possible to the town in the fork of a busy road junction and prevented from any additional penetration eastwards by the "Avoiding Line" embankment which runs from north to south at this point. York Road had its own signal box until 1934 when it was removed from the site to become a replacement for Thrybergh junction at the Swinton end of the Silverwood branch after an 04 2-8-0 had run away down the steep gradient and demolished the original building. York Road station was a single island platform, the arrival line coming alongside the departure face and being gained if required by means of a scissors crossover. A standard GC water tank and hoses featured at the outer end of the platform, on which the bolts could be seen in preparation to house the stanchions holding a roof that never materialised. North of the station lay the small yard, weigh office and small locomotive shed which for a time contained a forgotten contractor's engine swathed in sacking. A turntable well also appeared. Some distance away, facing the A1 road on its south side, was the stationmaster's house of similar design to the others elsewhere. South of the A1 road bridge was the Co-op dairy plant and bakery which required a short siding with access from both directions. It was of course possible to leave York Road and run either north or south by the triangular layout. In 1934 the southern spur was removed and the northern spur reduced to single line. Signalling here was a very vintage GC with some tall and doddery specimens of quite benign appearance, the up homes lasting until 1953. The station yard soon became the resort of various local concerns, including a petrol depot and scrap dealer.

The route ran straight, almost south-west through what was a pleasantly suburban district known as Anchorage Lane before turning due south to run parallel to the Doncaster "Avoiding Line". This occured for a short distance where the opportunity was taken to put in connecting spurs on a give and take basis, this point being Sprotborough junction at 1 mile 1,242 yds. The cabin was placed on the northerly, more gentle slope of the Don valley and from here the "Avoiding Line" and the Joint line on its right ran across embankments to cross the Don and bury themselves in the steep southern slope, the former line joining the parent route to Mexborough at Hexthorpe junction and passing over the Joint line in cutting. Some quite expensive engineering works took place here; the Joint line itself lay in a deep cutting

A coal train pulling out of Markham Main sidings.   G. Warness

between Hexthorpe and Warmsworth at 1 mile 1,432 yds. Near Sprotborough junction were quite capacious stables for the Logan and Hemingway horses used in the construction of the line. Complementary to the substantial lattice girder bridge of the "Avoider" was the smaller structure of the Joint Line carried on tubular columns at a somewhat lower level. Today a third bridge has been added, that of the A1(M) trunk route which crosses the river a little higher up. Sprotborough junction box had 44 levers, again an odd figure, of which all but five were used. A nearby wartime ammunition factory required a connection to the down road on the Joint line. An interesting situation was encountered at the junction as the down Joint and up "Avoiding Line" and corresponding up Joint and down "Avoiding Line" were in the same direction respectively. Thus, what was down on the "Avoiding Line" was in fact up on the Joint and vice-versa—all rather confusing in the train register.

Several bridges and the deep cutting were threaded to bring the Joint line to Warmsworth, the junction for a further colliery, Yorkshire Main, to which a double line ran south-east. Below on the left, just before the pointwork, a familiar style of house indicated that a station might be found here—in fact platforms and a footbridge did exist—for a very short time after the Great War. Warmworth junction was, after Bullcroft junction, the busiest point on the system at one time. The cabin had 48 levers. Through the colliery yard connection could be made with the Dearne Valley line of the L&Y which passed beneath the H&B and GC from west to east. Sidings at Warmsworth were grouped according to use, those for mineral traffic being on the same side as the cabin (up), the local freight yard being on the opposite side to which an approach led up from the main road below. Before it is forgotten, mention must be made of what was almost a three level crossing where the Doncaster to Edlington road was crossed by the DV, to be crossed in turn by the Joint line colliery branch. From the roadway if one were lucky one might see the L&Y 2-4-2T and coach, or even the motor train, emerging from beneath the colliery line, with an 04 waiting for the "right away" on the curve above—nostalgia indeed!

Beyond Warmsworth the line ran first up its most severe gradient of 1 in 94, and then by a long succession of cuttings and embankments to cover the long 4 miles 1,241 yds. to the junction with the GC, H&B and Midland Joint line from Thrybergh Jc. at Braithwell, a simple double bifurcation of "Y" shape, but with no less than three crossovers, one in each arm. Probably because of the cutting and curvature, the cabin was placed at right angles to the running within the fork. As far as is known only one other cabin, at Inverness, had this unusual siting. The M18 motorway now passes almost over the site of the junction. At 1,704 yds. south of Braithwell the tripartite Joint line led to Hellaby Siding near Maltby where much military hay traffic was handled during the Great War period, and which was noteworthy in that no less than three stop signals were provided in the up direction. Next came Thurcroft Sidings at 2 miles 463 yds. from Hellaby, and thus good access was given to the colliery there from all quarters. The sidings at Thurcroft were on the down side with the pit itself.

Chapter Nine. Joint Line Operation

Mineral workings on the Hull and Barnsley and Great Central Joint line were never very heavy and were generally considered as being in two divisions, the GC working traffic south of Bullcroft junction which was a sort of focal point and the H&B dealing with the rest of the system north of Bullcroft. However, records show that an H&B pilot engine from Bullcroft shed worked the yard at York Road until August 1926. It is also certain that H&B trains would work as far south as Warmsworth, possibly until North Eastern influence and policies made themselves felt. On May 8th, 1924, Driver Walter Williams of Cudworth received a cut over the left eye due to banging his head against the cab of ex H&B tank No. 2489 when it was propelling 46 empty wagons into Yorkshire Main colliery yard. The assembly came into rough contact with other stationary wagons. The GC did not normally penetrate north of Bullcroft junction where there could be seen at work engines of both companies and sometimes, by way of compromise, the tanks which, though built for the Lancashire Derbyshire and East Coast Railway, an over-ambitious constituent of the GC, were nevertheless sold to the H&B.

Traffic from Bullcroft pit would be moved via the single line route to the junction sidings in small trips as required to wait for making up into full loads. During the immediate post-nationalisation period no full train loads were shown timetabled from Skellow junction. Towards the end of the line's life Bullcroft's output would leave by the easier West Riding and Grimsby route. To Bullcroft junction from Hull came the trains of wooden pit props which were once so frequently seen and are now almost forgotten. These were stacked by the locomotive shed and the empty wagons could then be used for loads of coal. In 1948 a pickup train left Hull (Neptune Street) at 7.45 a.m., arriving at Bullcroft junction at 11.45 a.m. After shunting for an hour the working returned to Springhead. This was at that time the only booked working along the H&B section of the Joint line and was often worked by a venerable A7 4-6-2T or J21 0-6-0, both of unmistakable NE lineage. The home signals at the north end of the junction were three in number on a splendid bracket. Principal mineral workings were headed by the H&B 0-8-0s and six-coupled types. In LNER days O4s and Q6s were frequently seen, while during the last few years of running the ubiquitous WD 2-8-0s had sole charge of operations, taking some loads direct from Skellow junction to Hull. In connection with the merry-go-round coal train operations to Thorpe Marsh power station, to which a spur was laid in the '60s, the single line from Bullcroft junction enjoyed an Indian summer even after the old main route to the north was discarded, the junction box continuing, however, to log the traffic. On 24th July, 1968, to quote a typical day, the following traffic reached Thorpe Marsh at 6.50, 9.40, 9.50, 10.05, 13.45, 14.05. 1450, 17.55 and 1905.

Where the "Avoiding Line" and the Joint line came closest together at Sprotborough junction it was possible to pass traffic from one to the other, which caused the author when a youngster living close by much concern, as he was able to see multifarious "messing about" and hear much whistling but was unable to fathom it all out. Then came the day in 1946 when he was brave enough to take a walk down the Joint line over the Don to the cabin and spend the first of many happy sessions observing some fascinating signalling and traffic movements under the kindly and efficient eye of Mr. Sid. Lightfoot, then well over sixty years of age.

The "Avoiding Line" was, and still is, used as a relief route for freight traffic not concerned with Doncaster running through from Hull, Scunthorpe and Grimsby in the east, to Mexborough and beyond in the west, and vice-versa. In those days the prime daily freight was a working between Woodford Halse and Hull. Permissive block working was used, trains being allowed to draw up one behind the other after being cautioned on passing the cabin by the showing of a green hand-signal held steady. On this line as many as five trains might be seen on occasion waiting nose to tail to climb the 1 in 100 up to Hexthorpe junction on the main line. The box in rear was Bentley junction, where trains gain the "Avoiding Line" by a flying junction. For difficult cases a banking engine was available at Sprotborough junction, but more of that anon. Working at the junction was perhaps not too unusual but was nevertheless very interesting and worth setting down in some detail while memory still serves. Operators of model railways will find the movements of interest.

On summer Saturdays absolute block working was put into force, this being to pass through certain holiday passenger trains not booked to stop at Doncaster (Central). These trains were hauled by a motley selection of motive power, including "Directors", J11s single or in tandem, B7s and, in the latter days, B1s. On Sundays the junction was switched out, but both passenger and freight trains continued to use the line. Traffic from the Joint line to the south and from Yorkshire Main colliery (Warmsworth) was routed three ways at Sprotborough junction—to the Hull or Scunthorpe direction via Bentley junction, via Mexborough towards Rotherham and Sheffield or Wath; and towards Doncaster GC reversing at Hexthorpe junction, chiefly for locomotive coal supplies. After 1939 nothing appeared to pass straight up or down the Joint line, the bulk of Bullcroft coal output routed via the GC and H&B going northwards to the H&B proper. In 1948 two trains ran via Sprotborough junction to Bullcroft junction off the "Avoiding Line", one of these being of special note in that it came from Worksop at 6.30 a.m. via Brancliffe junction to Braithwell, then via Silverwood to Thrybergh junction and the GC proper instead of directly through Warmsworth. Four trains of empties ran to Warmsworth, two of which reversed direction at the junction. Similar return workings took place.

The diagram given herewith should be considered in relation to the movement of coal traffic. As will be seen the cabin had 44 levers, most of which were in use, and up to about 1950 the installation was almost entirely vintage GC dating from its completion in 1916. There were four fine pairs of signals on high brackets. One of these, signal No. 13, lived up to its nomenclature by being wayward and often refusing to return to danger, causing the signalman to leave the box to coax it back again. Yorkshire Main coal for Bentley junction eastwards was usually given a good run off the falling gradient with the relevant points and signals 25 and 5 pulled off in good time. Distants 10 and 36 were not normally used. Loads of coal bound for Doncaster GN (Hexthorpe) were brought to a stand at the home signals, and if of thirty loaded wagons or less were drawn over points Nos. 27 and 29 to be propelled over No. 38 crossover and thence all the way up to Hexthorpe junction. If the load exceeded more than 30 "on" then the banking engine which was stationed between points 18 and 19—forming a potential danger to the unprotected adjacent running lines—ran forward over No. 18 points and attached itself to the leading brake van of the train. After the exchange of

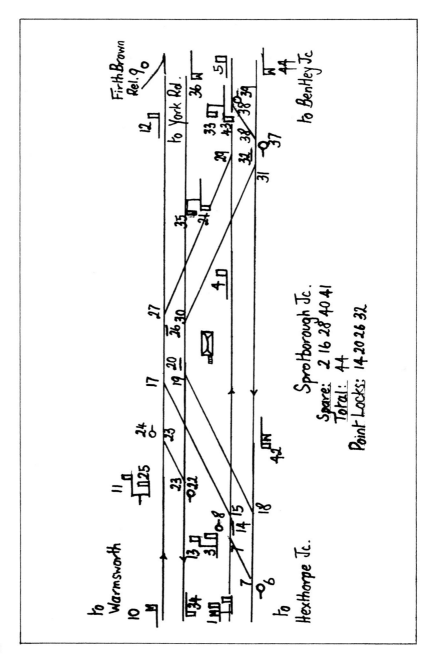

the double crow whistles the procession would get on the move, only to have to stop perhaps halfway up the gradient at Hexthorpe junction's outer home signal. Having cleared the latter junction, the train would then run forward down into the goods lines bound for Doncaster and the banker would return to base, regaining its normal position by using crossover road No. 7.

Incidentally, drivers of trains with through loads on the "Avoiding Line" would request banking assistance when passing Sprotborough junction box, either by whistling furiously at their approach, or by leaning right out of the cab and banging their fits one on top of the other—was this only found in GC practice, one wonders? Certainly it had its effect on the banking engine crew who left their cards in the box and sprinted out to render assistance. If they were slow off the mark and Hexthorpe had managed to clear the signals right through the train often managed to struggle to the top before the banker had made any contact with the tail end!

Most interesting of all were the loads worked from Yorkshire Main to Mexborough and beyond, for engine and brake van had to exchange ends. First the train, on arrival at No. 25 home signal, was drawn over Nos. 27 and 29 points to a position beyond No. 38 crossover. Then the train was propelled over this crossover up to the starting signal 42; the engine was uncoupled, ran back over No. 38 points, and went past its own train wrong line and over No. 7 crossover. When this had been reset, a green flag signal was exchanged for a whistle, the engine crew drew back on to the brake van which they collected, returned to beyond No. 6 ground signal and then back

Maltby Station.

across No. 7 points at great speed, usually fly shunting the brake at about 30 mph to a position well beyond No. 38 crossover—very well beyond if the guard was at all tardy with the brake wheel! Having dismissed the brake, as it were, the engine returned over No. 7 points, backed on to the wagons and propelled back over No. 38 points wrong line to right line to await the clear signal in the reverse direction via No. 39 ground signal. If the guard's van had disappeared into the distance, then of course the whole train had to be pushed along until contact was re-established with the wandering brake van. Sometimes the latter would come to a convenient halt by the Newton Hotel. In retrospect it seems amazing that such procedure was carried out quite frequently on heavily used lines. Much depended on the signalman's memory and commonsense; there was no track circuiting at Sprotborough and it would have been so easy to forget the loose brake van on the up line and pass a through train on to Bentley.

All this was enacted four or five times daily with the loaded trains, the empties in the opposite direction usually being propelled up to Warmsworth. While the signalman walked from one end of the frame to the other, carrying out the 21 lever movements necessary and keeping an eye on the through traffic piling up in block in both directions, the crew of the banking engine would be sitting in the cabin taking their ease unless the 04, Q4 or J11 looked as if in need of eventual rear-end assistance.

The banking engine was supplied by Mexborough shed and came on station at 6.30 a.m., usually being a J11 or N5 or L3 tank, or some old and venerable lady such as a B5 "Fish" engine. Nos. 5185, 5187 and 6072 of this class did turns after the last war, and on one occasion the shed turned out a tired old D9 No. 6016. Never did one see a "Director" on the turn, though these engines were used by Mexborough for the humblest tasks such as shunting the Warmsworth Lime Sidings. *Prince Henry, Edwin A. Beazley, Mons* and *Zeebrugge* spent many hours on this duty during the last war, should anyone have ever wondered at that particular time where they disappeared to!

At about 10.30 a.m. the banking engine ran to Hexthorpe Top Yard from whence it collected and propelled a shortish train of mixed freight, usually including petrol tanks, up to the junction, then down the "Avoiding Line" and over Nos. 14 and 17 points to the terminal yard at York Road, leaving there after a reasonable interval with a similar load and getting back on banking station by about 3.30 p.m. Should banking difficulties occur in absentia, such as the frequent post-war lunchtime stalling of a heavy Hull-Woodford freight headed by a Q6 or a B16 at its ultimate gasp, Sprotborough would ring Doncaster for a pilot and, after a decent lapse of time, up would come a breathy J52 doing at least 50mph, almost invariably with five or six men clinging to her flanks, for some non-apparent reason looking like a Keystone Cops fire engine. Perhaps they all liked the chance of a trip out! On at least one occasion the small pilot could not have been available as the main line pilot was sent. This was a GN "Atlantic" of all things, invariably very clean. The engine was one of two always available at Doncaster, and stood ready for action on the north turntable off the end of No. 5 platform. The crew passed the time in "B" box but had to keep going out to turn their charge to face the direction in which the next important express would run through, a busy job on summer Saturdays, but necessary with the engine failures rife after the war. No record was kept as to what was done with the "Atlantic" when expresses were due in both directions at the same time!

No. 63914 comes off the north end of the South Yorkshire Joint Line at Kirk Sandall Jc. A.J. Clarke

After 1948 the York Road turn was run earlier, the return working being completed by about one o'clock to allow the engine to return to banking duties. At about ten each evening, or whenever the box closed, the banker would run light to Doncaster West Yard to pick up a late goods for Mexborough. Until the formal banking was abandoned in the late fifties, B1s did the duties, including 61195, then 1195 in green livery, while on some occasions Doncaster shed provided the engine both before and after the war, often awarding the job to reshopped engines. Thus, one day a "Sandringham" actually put in an appearance, while for a short period immediately after its construction the pioneer L1 2-6-4T, then No. 9000 in apple green livery, served its time as Sprotborough banker. Usually, though, Doncaster would send out tired old GN 0-6-0s which were hardly able to propel themselves, let alone an incapacitated freight train. For many years a J6 0-6-0 used to work the evening train from the glassworks sidings at Kirk Sandall, either running via the "Avoiding Line" or directly through Doncaster to Hexthorpe junction. Usually a short train but with some heavy trestle wagons for plate glass, this run was known locally as "Pilks" for reasons which can easily be derived in view of the nature of the merchandise carried. During a high wind on one occasion the train was brought to a stand on the embankment while the crew descended to the Don to retrieve several sheets which had come adrift from the loads.

65

Latterly Sprotborough junction cabin stood rather forlorn and was only opened as required to pass through the Hexthorpe-York Road working. However, vandals did their worst and the box "died" in a fire in February 1973. The "Avoiding Line" is, however, as busy as ever, the diesel engines making little of the gradient which formerly caused so much interest.

York Road terminus was shunted by Hull and Barnsley engines until August 1926, when the locomotive depot at Bullcroft junction was closed, the operation of the Hexthorpe working to the yard being in the hands of Mexborough GC crews and their engines which also did the Sprotborough junction banking duty. From the changeover Doncaster did from time to time send along an engine and crew to work the turn. A note the author has shows a J3 0-6-0 covering the working in June 1930. During the 1939-45 war the former GC L3 tank engines, that ungainly but efficient breed of 2-6-4Ts, handled the banking and pick-up work. No. 5364 was a regular visitor. A now retired driver-enthusiast from Doncaster shed very kindly supplied the results of a well-spent boyhood logging engines appearing at York Road. The following H&B pilots were observed there:-

Saturday, 26th November, 1921:	Domeless 0-6-2T No. 107	11a.m.
Saturday, 31st December, 1921:	" " No. 110	4p.m.
Saturday, 25th March, 1922:	" " No. 108	4.30p.m.
Friday, 30th June, 1922:	" " No. 15	
Saturday, 21st April, 1923:	Domed " No. 97	
Saturday, 24th June, 1924:	" 0-6-0 No. 3081	
Monday, 30th June, 1924:	Domeless 0-6-0 No. 2417	
Monday, 16th August, 1926:	" 0-8-0 No. 2512	

As mentioned, the shed at Bullcroft junction closed in August 1926, so that the 0-8-0 could well have been the last H&B engine to work York Road yard.

Not to be outdone, the author found a fragment of his own spotting days—namely a particular day, 18th April, 1945—when for some reason or other the number of wagons, most of them at that time privately owned, passing Hexthorpe junction was counted. Fortunately the engine numbers were also recorded, so that some pleasant images can be invoked, as of No. 238 of Class D49 loping by with five bogies on the Hull-Liverpool (Central), of K3 No. 4007 passing down the "Avoiding Line" with 23 wagons on, and B5 4-6-0s Nos. 6072 and 5187 of Mexborough shed trundling coal trains about. "Directors" 5437 and 5438, probably from Darnall, were abroad on passenger workings on that day, but D11 No. 5503 of Mexborough very humbly brought 20 wagons of lime into the Top Yard. The Sprotborough banker of the day was an N2 0-6-2T No. 4726; thus Doncaster was having one of its periodic takeovers.

The York Road-Hexthorpe turn was the final spark of life on the whole of the Joint Line. Workings between Warmsworth and Braithwell were totally abandoned in 1942 when both running lines were blocked by the storage of rakes of crippled rolling stock, war victims awaiting repair. The down road from York Road to Bullcroft and beyond through to Snaith was used for the same forlorn purpose, giving the line a particularly abandoned air. Gaps were left wherever crossings intervened and to provide fire breaks. A start was made on moving the cripples in 1948, a pathetic sight since in some cases the wheels would not turn, but just slid along.

Of the passenger services on the GC and H&B Joint line little can be said unless one indulges in speculation since, as far as is known, no passenger stock ever traversed the line outside the odd enthusiasts' special performing the last rites. Possibly the idea of things was to have a service of local trains running from Carlton on the H&B main line, calling at the three intermediate stations to run into the terminus at York Road. The locomotive for these trips could have been a tank based at Bullcroft junction shed, or perhaps an engine could have run out from Hull (Springhead); possibly the idea was to run through services along the line from Hull (Cannon Street). York Road, being a terminus, would no doubt have called for a change of engine, possibly a 4-4-2T of GC origin from Mexborough shed, as in any event the running of the train would be reversed on leaving by the southern end of the triangle. Unless the rather pointless exercise was to run the train out over the "Avoiding Line" at Sprotborough and on to the GC proper onwards to Mexborough, the train would have only the intermediate station at Warmsworth before facing a considerable mileage without any stop until Anston, on the GC and Midland Joint line in the vicinity of Shireoaks was reached. This was hardly a rational proposition, though certainly no more unrealistic than the siting of most of the stations.

Snaith and Pollington lay on a good road running from east to west but was situated at some distance from both villages, the former being the larger but already having its own well-placed L&Y station giving a reasonable service to Goole and Wakefield. Both Balne and Heck, on the GN main line, offered a train service of sorts from both places for those wishing to visit Doncaster, Selby, York or beyond. Sykehouse was a small, remote village which might well have depended on the line if it had developed as planned; as it was, the nearest thorough-going station at Moss on the GN main line was four miles away and a local bus service reigned supreme. Thorpe-in-Balne was just as remote and much smaller, the nearest active railway station being 4½ miles to the south-east at Barnby Dun. Speculation prompted the siting of the above three stations, and where it was hoped that development would follow the coming of the line, none did. York Road was more suitably placed and might well have better for itself had the support of its approach roads been more useful. Doncaster town centre could be reached on foot in about 15 minutes, while the trams to and from Bentley and Woodlands passed the yard.

Warmsworth station lay to the south-west of Doncaster quite close to the Yorkshire Main colliery yard. Near it lay the small village of Warmsworth, already linked to the town by tram, and the large colliery village of New Edlington. Thus, the catchment area was promising, except that the potential passengers never had anywhere to go from the station. Possibly the concern had at the back of its mind the idea of running a service from here round to York Road for local passengers, but when presented with a nearby tram ride which was cheap and quick the choice was unfortunately obvious.

A legend put about by Joint line signalmen is that of the race special which ran from Hull to York Road in September 1919, alas without any positive confirmation, though it is delightful to imagine a domeless H&B 4-4-0 coming down the bank from the Bullcroft direction to swing round the curve into the island platform, its mixed rake of four-wheelers crammed with hopeful punters. Certainly it would have reached Doncaster by a more direct route than the customary one adopted by H&B race specials—out to Carlton, then by the spur from Gowdall junction to Hensall and Knottingley (L&Y) and round the sharp curve there on to the GN via Askern and Shaftholme junction. After 1946 the LNER considered upgrading the whole line as a trunk route for freight between Hull and the North Midlands via Worksop. This would have provided a speedy and convenient passenger link between North Humberside and points such as Nottingham, singularly free of complicated junctions and delaying cross traffic.

Sykehouse Station, with platforms but no buildings . . . . Collection C.T. Goode

Chapter 10. The West Riding and Grimsby Line

The West Riding and Grimsby Railway was a partnership of the Great Northern and Great Central companies; indeed, the GC never seemed to miss a chance of casting its net wherever possible, in this case in the direction of the important county town of Wakefield, whence a line led south-eastwards from the Westgate station. It passed through stations at Sandal, Hare Park, Nostell (from which place a triangular junction went off to Stairfoot, near Barnsley), Hemsworth and South Elmsall to Adwick junction at 16 miles. From this junction via Carcroft & Adwick-le-Street the WR&G led in to the principal GN line through Doncaster, at Marshgate junction. This route was opened in February 1866 and later stations on the line were at Hampole and Bentley Crossing, both wooden halts. Running due east from Adwick junction a second arm, opened in November 1866, extended for seven miles to Stainforth junction on the GC main line from Doncaster to Grimsby. From Skellow junction near to Adwick junction a curve ran round into Carcroft station, thus effecting a triangular layout having Adwick junction as the western point. Skellow junction also governed Bullcroft colliery yard on the north side and lay at the end of the single line branch from the GC and H&B Joint line at Bullcroft junction, a youngster which only appeared on the scene in 1916. Alterations at Skellow caused by the arrival of the line demanded a new signal box, and for many years both old and new cabins existed at the site, facing each other. The single line crossed the WR&G by a substantial girder bridge, having climbed up on the northern side. The GC and H&B proper crossed the WR&G shortly after the latter had bridged the GN main line near its northern end at Shaftholme junction. Here, opportunity was taken to build a north to east spur linking the two lines and giving NE trains access to Scunthorpe and Grimsby. To accommodate the connection a signal box was constructed at Applehurst junction. The canal which runs parallel to the river Don was crossed by a swing bridge having its own cabin adjacent, and at ¼ mile east of this came the only intermediate station on the section, Bramwith, opened post-1869 and originally named Barnby Dun, situated roughly on the route of the old South Yorkshire Railway which passed from north to south. Sidings to a maltings on the southern side of the line, and a small cabin controlling a fairly busy level crossing, completed the station scene here. Stainforth junction was soon reached, where a large brick water tower was situated in the fork to supply water to trains requiring refreshment on entering or leaving the branch.

Gradients on the Adwick junction to Stainforth section of the line were fairly easy and the most prominent engineering feature was the swing bridge over the canal where it ran parallel to the Don. This structure was replaced by a modern fixed span about 1955. At the bridge and at nearby Bramwith station was to be found a crop of vintage GN somersault signals used in the thorough-going "belt and braces" manner of the company concerned. Bramwith cautioned trains approaching from Stainforth with no less than three distant signals, plus Don Bridge cabin's distant, thus giving ample warning of the swinging span which was at times left open to river traffic, deliberately of course. The somersault signal was evolved by the GN after the disastrous accident of 1876 at Abbot's Ripton when snow choked the slot of one of the original types of semaphore signal, leaving it in a false "clear" position. With the somersault the arm was centrally pivotted, swinging clear of the post to around 60 degrees and leaving the spectacle glasses to perform as normally. In later years the bearings of the arms became worn, so that they could hardly ever be found horizontal, and when pulled off often reached the vertical or even beyond. Each signal thus displayed a certain individuality and a jaunty or ramshackle appearance. The unusual impact was often enhanced by the spectacle and lamp being housed lower down the post than the arm. At the west end of Bramwith the starter and home signal for each direction were combined on one post at exactly the same height and were back to back. The respective lamp glasses appeared lower down the post at different levels while, to complete the assemblage, the lattice post carried a fixed distant arm for the bridge cabin, plus its yellow light which was again lower down the post. To complete the irregularity no ladder was provided, the lamps being wound up and down on a chain. To control traffic GN style somersault distants fitted with GW style slow line rings were provided on lattice posts in each direction.

The West Riding and Grimsby line was an obviously successful route with a purpose which could be easily exploited, unlike some of the earlier projects mentioned hitherto. Undoubtedly the Applehurst junction to Joan Croft junction spur of 1877 letting in the NE was a great asset and the timetable of 1948 shows several freight services using the connection, there being two running from York (Dringhouses) to Grimsby and Frodingham, with three in the reverse direction. One interesting service was an additional vegetable train running from Algakirk, between Spalding and Boston, at 1.30p.m., passing Applehurst junction at 7.30p.m. to arrive at Newcastle at 12.12a.m. Booked freight services running across the route from Wakefield to Stainforth were roughly three in number in each direction, those running east generally completing their runs at Frodingham, while those in the opposite direction terminated at Ardsley where was situated a large marshalling yard and locomotive depot. Additional shorter workings of interest included one from New Clee to Bullcroft colliery (Skellow junction) where the empty wagons arrived at the ungodly hour of 2.48a.m. SX. On three days a week Frodingham sent a train of empties to Brodsworth colliery via the branch from Castle Hills, reaching there at 2.09p.m.

Passenger workings on the line were heavy and regular on the main section, which was of course part of the principal route from Leeds to Doncaster, although Bradshaw divides this route into two, that section from Wakefield (Westgate) to Leeds (Central) being shown as a branch and appearing in a separate table from the rest of the GN East Coast route section. From the WR&G station at Wakefield with its dominant clock tower, slow trains could depart and dally at the seven stations en route before reaching Doncaster at 20 miles. In 1937 an island platform was opened at Fitzwilliam, between Hemsworth and Nostell. The station buildings at Carcroft and at South Elmsall were of an extremely distinctive and pleasant design, with hipped roofs and a suggestion of turrets. South Elmsall served a thriving mining community and could, in 1914, offer the following services which are roughly representative of the whole route:

Departures for Doncaster:
8.05a.m.; 9.45a.m. (SO starts); 9.52a.m.; 12.24p.m.; 1.52p.m. (to King's Cross arr. 6.02p.m.); 3.01p.m.; 4.01p.m.; 5.51p.m. (arr. King's Cross 9.25p.m.); 6.47p.m.; 8.23p.m.; 9.19p.m.; 11.13p.m. (arr. King's Cross 3.24a.m.); 12.09a.m. (Th, SO).

Departures for Leeds:
7.58a.m.; 9.28a.m.; 11.31a.m.; 11.40a.m.; 1.30p.m. (to Huddersfield and Halifax); 2.38p.m.; 4.02p.m. SO; 5.21p.m.; 6.17p.m.; 7.57p.m.; 9.10p.m. (to Huddersfield and Halifax); 9.47p.m.; 10p.m.; 11.02p.m. (SO).

Of the two interesting station buildings South Elmsall has recently been demolished after de-staffing, leaving Carcroft, closed a long time ago, to survive in private hands. Below are departures from South Elmsall for 1974, to compare with the earlier ones above:

Departures for Doncaster:
8.34a.m. (8.39a.m. SO); 9.35a.m. (SO to Cleethorpes); 9.45a.m. (SO to Yarmouth); 1.34p.m.; 2.47p.m.; 4.13p.m. (SO to Lincoln); 5.14p.m. (to Cleethorpes); 5.44p.m.; 6.39p.m.; 9.47p.m. (SO); 10.51p.m. (to King's Cross).

Departures for Leeds:
6.57a.m.; 7.57a.m.; 9.27a.m. (SO to Blackpool); 9.33a.m.; 10.38a.m.;

Two class 37s pass down the "Avoiding Line" across the Don with a coal train. Beyond can be seen the H&B and GC Joint line bridge.   *T.G. Flinders*

11.53a.m. (SO from Cleethorpes); 1.15p.m. (from King's Cross); 2.40p.m. (from Cleethorpes); 2.54p.m. (SO from Skegness); 3.25p.m. (SO from Yarmouth); 5.46p.m.; 9.11p.m.

In 1914 there were three trains each way on Sundays; in 1974 there were no stopping trains.

The section of the WR&G line from Adwick junction to Stainforth never supported any sort of local train service, and it is not clear as to why a station was ever constructed at Bramwith. The usual excuses such as hopeful speculation could be made, but the area has remained stubbornly agricultural in character. Bramwith village lay to the north of the line, about two miles away, the nearest village on that side being the smaller community of Thorpe-in-Balne. On the south side, however, lay Barnby Dun which had its own station on the nearby GC Grimsby line. No evidence has been found to show that passengers were ever dealt with at the station, though a small amount of goods traffic was handled. One feature of the line which was interesting was its use for through traffic by passenger services between Leeds. Bradford and the coast, there being in the early days a working leaving Leeds at nine in the morning, arriving at Cleethorpes at 11.16a.m. and leaving for the return trip of 77 miles at 3.20p.m., somewhat early for the buckets and spades one might suspect. After the 1939-45 war the service left Leeds at 8.10a.m., taking much longer in a round three hours to Cleethorpes, this probably due to the poor state of the track in the vicinity of Don Bridge. A similar Saturdays only working left Bradford at 8.40a.m. There was an untidy arrangement of departures from Cleethorpes at 1.40p.m. and 2.02p.m. SO; also a later return at 7.15p.m. SO to cater for the trippers. On three occasions in the week a service left Cleethorpes at 9.10a.m., getting to Leeds at 11.52a.m., this presumably with shoppers in mind, though at the time nobody had thought of getting them home again except via a change at Doncaster. By 1957 this inadequacy had been realised and the service, now out of Cleethorpes at 9.23a.m. and through Bramwith at 11a.m., returned from Leeds at 4.13p.m. with a coast arrival at 7.12p.m. Needless to say, the modern timetable reverted to a situation where only the return train is direct, outward shoppers having to change at Doncaster except on Saturdays. Present policy is to run units between Leeds and Scunthorpe calling everywhere and reversing at Doncaster.

Haulage on the cross-country trains was usually in the hands of K2s and K3s, D10s, D11s and latterly B1s before the advent of diesel multiple units. Similar steam locomotives had a share of the stopping train workings on the Doncaster to Leeds service. Occasionally, a Gresley Pacific would find itself running in on a couple of coaches on these trains, while perhaps a rather incongruous Jubilee was to be seen ending its days on such a train from Leeds Central before that station—and steam—were to disappear for ever. Shortly after the end of the last war an ex GC 4-6-0 of Ardsley shed caused a furore by dropping a connecting rod or something equally drastic when passing beneath the road bridge at Carcroft, fortunately without loss of life. It was always a pleasant sight to run into Stainforth on the 5.08p.m. slow from Doncaster to Hull and see the Leeds-Cleethorpes train waiting at the WR&G water crane on the left, the fireman on the tender shovelling down the coal as the driver tinkered round the wheels with his oil can. The train always followed the Hull man in to Stainforth and gave a connection to Scunthorpe and beyond.

The WR&G was useful diversionary route in times of trouble. In 1933 the GN main line between Doncaster and Shaftholme was flooded, necessitating all services to and from the north passing round the Applehurst junction spur and calling at Stainforth, where they had to reverse. More recently, as when a bridge was renewed over the Don at Marshgate, trains from Hull and Cleethorpes gained Doncaster via the reverse curve at Carcroft, running via Bramwith and Stainforth junction.

Today, the WR&G is used much as formerly, with the important addition of Thorpe Marsh power station which has its own siding connection to the facilities laid out for "merry-go-round" train operation, this installation being south of the line near Applehurst junction. After deliberation, this traffic was taken away from the GC and H&B Joint line, now abandoned, including its branch to Skellow junction.

Chapter 11. The Dearne Valley Railway

The Dearne Valley Railway, covered fully in a separate work by the author, was a private company largely in name only, since its major officials, including its chairman and the traffic superintendent, Mr. Marriott, were shared with the parent Lancashire and Yorkshire Railway. Authorised by an Act of 6th August, 1897, it was a main line of just over seventeen miles, plus additional siding mileage, the route running from the Hull and Barnsley Railway at Brierley junction near to the Cudworth yards, and then generally south eastwards to a point in the vicinity of Doncaster where traffic could be dispersed readily to the Great Northern and Great Eastern systems. As was the usual practice of the time, the construction of the whole line was divided into sections, as follows:- Railways 1 and 2 from Brierley junction to Thurnscoe six miles, tendered for by Naylor Bros. in 1898 and 1900; Railway No. 3 from Thurnscoe to Denaby, tendered for by Gates and Hogg in 1903; Railway No. 4 from Denaby to Black Carr, won by H. Lovatt Ltd. in 1904. The last contained the heavier works, the first mentioned being relatively free of difficulties. The line was opened in easy stages from the Brierley junction end, traffic moving from Cadeby colliery early in 1906. The heavy embankments and cuttings to the east of this point delayed through running until March 1909, the various spurs and connections at Black Carr being fitted in and made ready by May 1909.

The features of the line are best described in detail by proceeding steadily from west to east, the return run being made perhaps more expediently on the push and pull passenger service. One suspects that the L&Y considered the DV to be part of the main system for operating purposes; they had constructed a line known as the Dearne Valley Junction Railway from the triangular junctions at Crofton to Shafton junction, meeting the DV where it descended from the H&B. This line was opened in March 1905 and enabled coal traffic to be taken westwards off the DV and round the Crofton triangle in the opposite direction to the port of Goole. West-bound hauls of coal faced a couple of miles mainly at 1 in 100, though immediately after Ryhill Halt the descent was equally steep but of course favourable to them. The line crossed the GN and GC Joint line near Hare Park by a fine lattice girder bridge.

The DV when originally constructed was single line throughout, but after 1915 it was doubled from Shafton junction to Barnburgh and is better considered in its final form. At Brierley junction a run of double track led southwards to the point at Shafton junction where the extension from Crofton junction joined in. There is evidence that a cabin existed on the spur, at Hiendley, giving access to a small colliery; certainly the block instrument at Brierley junction passing traffic on and off the DV was marked "Hiendley" and not "Shafton junction". The Hiendley cabin could have controlled the point where the spur ran into single line, which it undoubtedly did before reaching Shafton junction, where the cabin was placed in the fork. After Grimethorpe Halt the double track took in colliery sidings on the north side and a further larger set from the Grimethorpe and Ferrymoor collieries immediately after crossing the GC line from Stairfoot to the same yard. This latter line was also a single track, and from it a single line led back round parallel to the DV to run to Houghton Main colliery, encountered next to the south side of the line as the DV ran eastwards between the cabins of Grimethorpe Sidings and Houghton Sidings, both also on the south side. There was also an additional down running line of about ¾ mile here, the only place on the DV where this was found. Houghton Main was served by the DV, GC and the nearby Midland main line from Sheffield to Leeds.

Close by Houghton colliery tip was Great Houghton Halt, handier for the colliery than for the village which was north of the line up a steep and winding lane. A mile or so further east was an important complex of lines in the

Goldthorpe area, the DV passing directly through Goldthorpe village in cutting and running south of Hickleton colliery. Viewed from the western end of the area, first came Thurnscoe junction cabin, from which point a double track spur led north to the Swinton and Knottingley Joint line passing under the DV at right angles a little further on. The spur would conveniently give NE trains access to Houghton Main colliery, and was of more use to that company during its existence than it would have been to the DV. The spur was opened in March 1905. Nearer to Goldthorpe, actually Highgate at this point, was Goldthorpe and Thurnscoe Halt, sporting—like all the other halts on the line—a shelter which was only the shell of an old coach, plus a couple of lamps and some sleepers to stand on. The S&K, as mentioned, passed beneath the DV at this point, while parallel to it but in a deeper cutting ran the Hull and Barnsley's Wath branch, the whole parcel of lines being neatly tied by a main road which crossed all three routes—a bridge-builder's dream, or nightmare. The DV bridge carrying the road was of a substantial girder construction of generous width able to carry the present-day roadway and its traffic. At Goldthorpe Halt a siding was put in to deal with pick-up freight, the outlet being controlled by Nicholas Lane box. A scrap merchant had taken over this siding during the last war. To add to the complication of railway thrusts in the area, from yet another cabin a little further east a spur ran in northwards between the S&K and H&B lines to tap Hickleton colliery. This section of the DV was particularly attractive because of the number of L&Y signals with miniature arms, as well as the miltifarious signal boxes, all with the typical long nameboard running along the front.

Moving east again along double track the sidings of Goldthorpe colliery were encountered on the north side, governed by a further cabin. Barnborough (sometimes spelled Barnburgh) colliery sidings were situated a mile or so further east, there being a wide loop giving access to them behind the cabin. Here was virtually the end of the doubling of the original line, though the up line continued as a long siding for a further ¼ mile or so to become a goods siding at Harlington Halt, a single platform on the north side. Both Harlington and Barnborough villages were suitably placed to provide passengers for the little halt which was well situated.

The line, which had been falling generally from Shafton junction, apart from a hump at Goldthorpe, pursued its single course down the Dearne valley, somewhat marshy and scrubby in character and subject to subsidence and flooding. This demanded the construction of a long embankment to Denaby at 9¾ miles from Shafton junction. Two crossings of the Dearne were made by bridges which needed deep foundations in their construction. Denaby was something of a non-starter in that it was sited in the middle of a marshy wilderness. The halt proclaimed itself as the Mecca—"Denaby, for Conisbrough and Mexborough", the furthest of these lying a mere 3½ miles away! Not surprisingly it was the first halt to close in 1949. The site was awkward, too, for the important purpose of tapping collieries thereabouts; however, the single line became double and two branches went off on the south side, one to Cadeby colliery and a longer one of about ¾ mile to Denaby Main which was opened on 4th August, 1906. This arm required a solid bridge across the river Don. At Denaby the smaller river Dearne runs into the Don which now runs generally west-east through a valley whose slopes are steepish and rise to about 600ft. on either side. Both Denaby and Cadeby collieries were situated on the north bank of the river and were served by the DV which was on the higher of two terraces above them, the lower one being occupied by

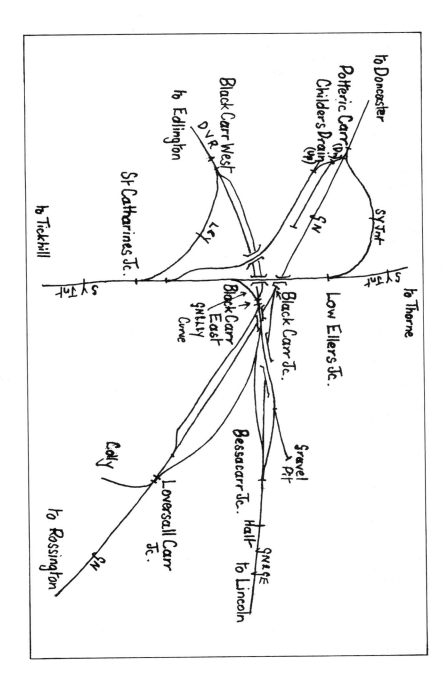

the South Yorkshire Junction Railway (H&B) running from Sprotborough and descending over the Don to Lowfield junction on the south side, situated on the GC main route from Doncaster to Mexborough. Needless to say, the GC formed the third party interested in the coal output of the two pits.

On leaving the area of Cadeby colliery the DV curved towards the south-east in cutting and crossed the H&B just before it entered its own tunnel, beyond which is a rather dusty and very obvious lime-processing plant. Immediately afterwards the DV crossed the GC, already in tunnel at a lower level, and then struck out boldly across the valley by its masterpiece, a viaduct of 21 blue brick arches, 1,525ft. long. At a height of 150ft. above the river was an underslung lattice girder span of 113ft. The whole structure which was built for double track but only ever used for a single line was opened in March 1909. A characteristic of the single line was that, for some reason, it was slewed on its passage over the bridge from the down to the up side which had an intriguing visual effect when viewed from above. Construction of the viaduct was carried out by means of an aerial rope-way across the river and the skilful use of wooden scaffolding. The river itself also played a part, a barge being used to float and raise the centre span into position by displacement. The line, which had climbed to the level viaduct, now fell into a deep magnesian limestone cutting beneath the Doncaster to Sheffield road at Butterbusk, and then curved more easterly to cross the GC and H&B Joint line, itself in deep cutting, before emerging in the area of Yorkshire Main colliery at Edlington Halt. The output of this pit was taken by the DV and the GC and H&B, possibly the former getting the lion's share. From Edlington Halt, placed on the single line with a siding off controlled by a ground frame, the line went into two at a passing loop which accommodated the spur from the colliery on the south side, governed by a smallish signal box with the sonorous name "Yorkshire Main Sidings Box".

From here the last mile or so is over the Doncaster "Carrs", the local name for flat marshy land rich in wild life of all kinds, to that most interesting place south-east of the town of Doncaster where the GN main line to London throws off, at Black Carr junction, what is in effect the older route via Gainsborough and Lincoln. The DV finished its run here and sent out flying junctions to both the lines, these complications being demanded by the GN to avoid the hold-ups that a standard junction would have imposed on its prime express traffic. Certainly it cost the DV a great deal of extra expense over and above the cost of a single turnout west of Black Carr junction which could have taken the traffic just as well. Four spurs of line, opened in May 1909, had to be built along with their earthworks on marshy terrain, these demanding two girder spans, one on the skew of 163ft. in length. The top layer of the railway "cake" at this point came in January 1909 when the SYJ passed across the other two concerns from north to south and was linked with the GN by a curving spur from Low Ellers junction to Potteric Carr junction. At the southern perimeter of the complex lines was St. Catherine's junction where three connections trailed in from the north. There was a spur round from the DV at Black Carr West giving access to all the collieries on the SYJ; and then also on the west side of the SYJ a nebulous single line connections with the down sidings by the GN at Childer's Drain. Inspection of St. Catherine's junction might lead one to suppose that points were never laid in for this connection, though the first twelve levers, being spare, were probably reserved for it. Childer's Drain cabin had an identical set of twelve spares. Possibly it was intended as part of a flying junction to the GN, of which the Low Ellers curve was to be the other arm. To the east of the SYJ a spur came round from Black Carr East, a DV cabin of some size which also controlled a run of sidings and the aforementioned flying junctions. The latter spur was constructed jointly by the L&Y and GN and served the NE constituent of the Joint Committee well in that it permitted them access to nearby Rossington colliery. During the whole of the time that the DV took coal from the SYJ territory, the western spur was used at St. Catherine's, loads from Armthorpe being handled in the same manner as those of the GN by being propelled to the junction. The eastern spur was little used, except that once a year a light engine from the LMS would appear loaded with officials who would beat the bounds, claiming territorial rights by running over it.

Mineral workings on the Dearne Valley line were always fairly heavy, and the doubling of the line in 1916 was justified. Much of the coal was fed into the West Riding, while some went via the Dearne Valley Junction line to Crofton and thence via Knottingley to Goole, a rather circuitous affair in some respects. The complex at the eastern end of the system enabled coal traffic to be worked off by the GN and GE companies through the Black Carr sidings, though one suspects that the volume of traffic never justified the expense of the layout. Coal trains were hauled by the small 0-8-0 tender engines of Aspinall's design with the characteristic low and straight wheel splashers and small tenders, or the LMS equivalent in the eight coupled engines built by Fowler between 1929 and 1932 with their big boilers and generally

The massive lattice girder span carrying the Dearne Valley line over the Great Northern main line at Black Carr Junction. T.G Flinders

THE NEW SCHEME

Following detailed study of transport needs South Yorkshire and West Yorkshire Passenger Transport Executives (in pursuance of the policies of their respective Passenger Transport Authorities) together with British Rail, are jointly planning a scheme to meet the following objectives:

Improving

ACCESS TO AND FROM – THE DEARNE TOWNS AREA – BOLTON, GOLDTHORPE AND THURNSCOE

RAIL LINKS BETWEEN SHEFFIELD, ROTHERHAM, WAKEFIELD AND LEEDS

THE ATTRACTIVENESS OF TRAIN TRAVEL TO AND FROM ROTHERHAM CENTRAL

Improving links to the Dearne Towns

The new train service provides travel opportunities from the Dearne Towns area to improve job prospects and access to leisure and shopping facilities.
For journeys to Rotherham and Sheffield the service complements the existing X91 bus service and provides passengers with a departure approximately every half hour to and from Sheffield.
Journey times by the new train service will be approximately half the equivalent bus journeys.
At present there are no direct bus services linking the Dearne Towns to Wakefield and Leeds. This new service brings both places within convenient travelling time – see the examples below.

From	To	(Approximate journey times – minutes)		
	Sheffield	Rotherham	Wakefield	Leeds
Bolton-on-Dearne	22	12	29	49
Goldthorpe	25	15	26	46
Thurnscoe	27	17	24	44

Ivatt 2.6.2T No. 41284 arrives at Edlington Halt in April 1951 (L&Y Dearne Valley section)   *C.T. Goode*

massive appearance. Wakefield shed had many of these machines and was indeed one of the last strongholds of steam in the north, having finally a stud of WD 2-8-0s to handle the mineral traffic.

One of the most interesting and certainly one of the most ramshackle passenger services in the whole area was that provided from Wakefield (Kirkgate) to Edlington Halt, proudly designated the station for Doncaster, with a footnote "for Balby." Warmsworth was in fact the nearer village, to which the trams ran from Doncaster, about 3½ miles away. Balby lay intermediately situated. As mentioned, there were five haults on the DV, each comprising an old coach body shell in varying degrees of decrepitude depending on the ingenuity of the local vandals, plus a sleepered platform at rail height. On the Dearne Valley Junction line, over which the service ran to gain access to Kirkgate station, were two further halts, at Ryhill 6½ miles from Wakefield, and just outside the locomotive depot before the end of the run was reached.

Basically, four return runs were operated on weekdays, plus an extra late service on Saturdays. In the latter days this had been reduced to two round trips with the addition of two shorter runs out to Goldthorpe and Thurnscoe only. The service began on 3rd June, 1912, employing one of the eighteen steam rail motors designed by Hughes for the L&Y and built between 1906 and 1911. Each consisted of a small 0-4-0T and saloon coach, the engine

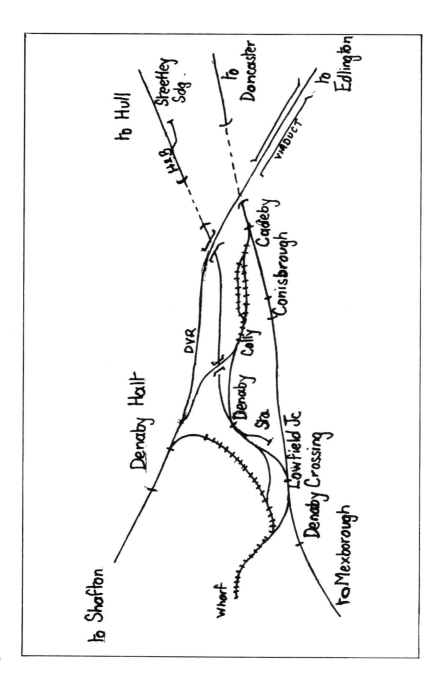

having a boiler pressure of 160lb., cylinders of 12″ x 16″ and a weight of 32 tons 14cwt. The tiny driving wheels were 3ft. 7ins. The coach, which possessed a single bogie at the outer end, rested its inner end on a pivot on the engine and was fitted with let-down steps controlled by the vacuum system, hence the absence of proper platforms at the halts. The rail motors, known as "Titanics", were used during the thirties and up to the outbreak of hostilities. No. 10616 performed for many years on the run; however, wartime lack of proper servicing began to take its toll and, as with other types of railcar where the power unit was virtually integrally built with the passenger section, the little Hughes units were regarded as "odd" and something of a nuisance cluttering up the depot awaiting repair. The carriage portion deteriorated, often due to the habit of cleaners and others to use it as somewhere to take a quick nap or as an impromptu canteen, and thus by 1948 only one survived to work the Blackrod-Horwich branch. By the middle of the war at least two of the ubiquitous 2-4-2Ts owned by the L&Y, Nos. 10650/6, were doing duty on the DV service using a steam rail motor coach which had acquired the necessary bogie from somewhere. The service was therefore now purely push and pull. The last of the 309 2-4-2Ts went in 1961, but the final weeks of the DV passenger service ended in glory of a kind in the hands of the new Ivatt tanks Nos. 41283/4 fitted for push and pull working and still utilising the original Hughes saloon coach. The last service ran on 9th September, 1951.

Dearne Valley Railway Passenger Services, 1925.

							SO	SO
		a.m.	a.m.	p.m.	p.m.	p.m.	p.m.	p.m.
Wakefield Kirkgate	dep:	8.10	10.25	1.05	3.28	6.05	9.30	9.45
Ryhill	dep:	8.28	10.43	1.23	3.46	6.23	9.48	10.03
Grimethorpe	dep:	8.36	10.51	1.31	3.54	6.31	9.56	10.11
Great Houghton	dep:	8.47	11.02	1.42	4.05	6.42	10.07	10.22
Goldthorpe & Thurn	dep:	8.52	11.07	1.47	4.10	6.47	10.12	10.27
Harlington	dep:	8.57	11.12	1.52	4.15	6.52	10.17	
Denaby	dep:	9.01	11.16	1.56	4.19	6.56	10.21	
Edlington for Balby	dep:	9.10	11.25	2.05	4.28	7.05	10.30	

							SO	SO
		a.m.	a.m.	p.m.	p.m.	p.m.	p.m.	p.m.
Edlington for Balby	dep:	9.13	11.28	2.12	4.35	8.15		10.36
Denaby	dep:	9.29	11.44	2.28	4.51	8.23		10.52
Harlington	dep:	9.34	11.49	2.33	4.56	8.28		10.57
Goldthorpe & Thurn	dep:	9.40	11.55	2.39	5.02	8.42	10.30	11.03
Great Houghton	dep:	9.45	12.00	2.44	5.07	8.47	10.38	11.08
Grimethorpe	dep:	9.56	12.11	2.55	5.18	8.58	10.50	11.19
Ryhill	dep:	10.05	12.20	3.04	5.27	9.07	10.59	11.28
Wakefield Kirkgate	dep:	10.20	12.35	3.19	5.42	9.22	11.15	11.43

The number of passengers conveyed on the trains was never great, especially as the line suffered from heavy bus competition throughout its length. Latterly, the setting up of a miners' welfare centre at Yorkshire Main gave the service a boost, especially on Saturdays when local sporting

There will soon be two routes between
Sheffield and Leeds

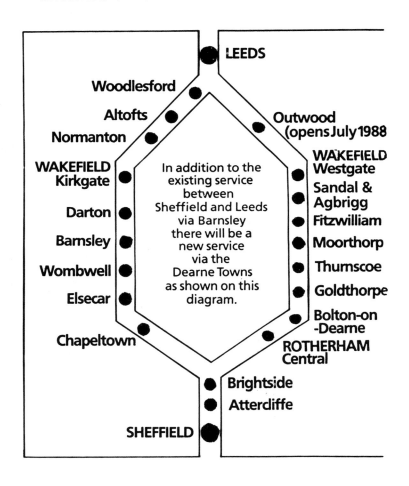

LEEDS

Woodlesford

Altofts

Outwood
(opens July 1988

Normanton

WAKEFIELD
Kirkgate

WAKEFIELD
Westgate

In addition to the
existing service
between
Sheffield and Leeds
via Barnsley
there will be a
new service
via the
Dearne Towns
as shown on this
diagram.

Sandal &
Agbrigg

Darton

Fitzwilliam

Barnsley

Moorthorp

Wombwell

Thurnscoe

Elsecar

Goldthorpe

Bolton-on
-Dearne

Chapeltown

ROTHERHAM
Central

Brightside

Attercliffe

SHEFFIELD

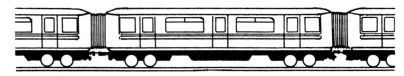

fixtures would bring supporters down from Goldthorpe and other stations. Tickets were issued on the train by the guard, the cheap day return fare for the total run being 4s 2d. Total running time each way was just over the hour if one was lucky. At times the handling of much more lucrative coal traffic led to heavy delays; even so the service was still more convenient and quicker to get from say, Goldthorpe to Wakefield than by going by bus which meant a change in Barnsley. Denaby Halt was just too remote from anywhere to be an asset and closed in January 1949. Possibly the most used halt served Ryhill, a largish village also having a station on the theoretically useful GC route from Barnsley to Leeds (Central) via Wakefield, both stations being close to the village. The GC route was good in theory in that it served three places of importance very readily, but was in fact badly graded, beset by coal traffic and had the problem of filtering in its trains to the busy Doncaster-Leeds line at Nostell. It died in the early thirties. To indicate the rail facilities offered to Ryhill at one time, the departures for both stations in 1916 are given. The run to Wakefield by GC trains took 12 minutes for the eight miles, while L&Y trains needed 13 minutes for six miles.

Ryhill GC dep (for Leeds): 8.34a.m. 11.44a.m. 2.19p.m. 4.56p.m. 6.57p.m. SO. 9.42p.m. 12.07a.m. SO.
Ryhill Halt L&Y dep (for Wakefield): 9.58a.m. 12.08p.m. 2.58p.m. 5.04p.m. 11.13p.m. SO.
The GC offered a much more lavish service of course, and their very late last train provides a nice touch.

On 4th July, 1966, a connection was put in at Houghton, north-west of the colliery, which brought down the DV route from both directions as spurs to the former Midland main line; thus, traffic could be worked off over this new route and the fate of the old push and pull line as a through passage was sealed. From Grimethorpe to Brierley junction and along the whole length of the Dearne Valley Junction, the line was closed completely, while the single line from Houghton through Goldthorpe to the colliery was left to serve the site. Running eastwards, the whole line was taken up right to Yorkshire Main sidings, and the Conisbrough viaduct stands derelict at the time of writing. From Yorkshire Main the line has been left as an outlet to St. Catherine's junction, mineral trains being propelled thence and reversing to run forward over the SYJ. The Black Carr flying junctions have been taken up, the bridges remaining for use in a modernisation scheme whereby trains can run both ways to the down side of the main line to or from Doncaster and gain or leave the correct line of running via the bridges which also provide fast access to the Lincoln line. Both Black Carr East and West boxes and the sidings are no more.

Dates for Station Closures in South Yorkshire

* Have been reopened

+ Probably

Ackworth	S&K	2.7.51
Askern	L&Y	27.948
Arksey	GN	5.8.52
Attercliffe	GC	26.9.27
Balne	NE	15.9.58
Barnby Dun	GC	4.9.67
Bawtry	GN	6.10.58
Beauchief	MR	2.1.61
Beighton	GC	1.11.54
Broughton Lane	GC	3.4.56
Crofton	L&Y	30.11.31
Carcroft	GN	6.11.67
Cudworth	MR	1.1.68
Darfield	MR	17.6.63
Dovecliffe	GC	7.12.53
* Dronfield	MR	2.1.67
Deepcar	GC	15.6.59
Denaby	H&B	1.2.03
Denaby Halt	L&Y	1.1.49
Ecclesfield West	MR	6.11.67
Finningley	GN/GE	11.9.61
* Fitzwilliam	WR&G	6.11.67
Frickley	S&K	6.8.53
Hampole	WR&G	7.1.52
Hare Park	GN	4.2.52
Hickleton	H&B	6.4.29
Hemsworth	GN	6.11.67
Hemsworth & Sth Kirkby	H&B	1.1.32
Healey	MR	+ 2.1.61
Haxey	GN/GE	2.2.59
Killamarsh Cen	GC	4.3.63
Killamarsh West	MR	
Kilnhurst Cen	GC	5.2.68
Kilnhurst West	MR	1.1.68

84

Kirk Smeaton	H&B	1.1.32
Medge Hall	GC	12.9.62
Moorhouse	H&B	6.4.29
Monk Bretton	MR	27.9.37
Moss	NE	6.8.53
Norton	L&Y	27.9.48
Neepsend	GC	28.10.40
Nostell	WR&G	29.10.51
Oughty Bridge	GC	15.6.59
Pickburn	H&B	1.2.03
Park Drain	GN/GE	7.2.55
Parkgate & Aldwarke	GC	29.10.51
Parkgate & Rawmarsh	MR	1.1.68
Rotherham Road	GC	5.1.53
Rotherham Westgate	MR	6.10.52
Rotherham Holmes	MR	6.10.52
Rossington	GN	6.10.58
Ranskill	GN	6.10.58
Royston & Notton	MR	1.1.68
* Sandal	WR&G	4.11.57
Scrooby	GN	14.9.31
Sandal & Walton	MR	+ 1.1.68
Sprotborough	H&B	1.2.03
Sharlston	L&Y	3.3.58
Sheffield Victoria	GC	5.1.70
Staincross	GC	22.9.30
Stairfoot	GC	16.9.57
Summer Lane	GC	29.6.59
Swinton Cen	GC	15.9.58
* Swinton Town	MR	1.1.68
Treeton	MR	29.10.51
Tinsley	GC	29.10.51
Unstone	MR	29.10.51
Upton & Nth Elmsall	H&B	1.1.32
Wath Cen	GC	26.9.59
Wath North	MR	1.1.68
Wath	H&B	6.4.29
Wincobank & M Hall	MR	2.4.56
Wentworth & HC	MR	2.11.59

Wombwell	GC	26.9.59
Woodhouse Mill	MR	21.9.53
Wortley	GC	2.5.55
Wadsley Bridge	GC	15.6.59
Womersley	L&Y	27.9.48
South Yorkshire Joint Line	GN/GC/L&Y/ NE/MR	2.12.29
Stairfoot to Tinsley	GC	7.12.53
Dearne Valley Railway	L&Y	10.9.51

BOOKED SHUNTING ENGINES 1948

Station or Yard	Depot from which Engine provided	Number or description of Pilot	Period required at Station or Yard	Particulars of Work
ALDAM JUNCTION	Mexboro' ..	No. I Marshalling	6.0 a.m. Monday to 11.30 p.m. Saturday	Marshals as required
		No. 2 Marshalling	7.0 a.m. to 6.0 p.m. Weekdays	„ „ „
BARNBY DUN..	Doncaster ..	No. I Marshalling	10.0 a.m. to 3.0 p.m. (SO) .. 12.0 noon to 6.0 p.m. (SX) ..	Marshals as required Afterwards works 6.7 p.m. Barnby Dun to Swinton L.M.R. (SX)
BARNSLEY, Top Yard	Barnsley ..	No. I Marshalling	6.0a. m. to12.50 p.m and 3.0 p.m. to 11.0 p.m. (SX) 6.0a.m. to 11.0 p.m.(SO)	Marshals as required
Pindar Oaks ..	„ ..	No. 2 „	6.30 a.m. to 10.0 p.m. Weekdays ..	„ „ „
BROUGHTON LANE	Darnall ..	No. I Marshalling	6.0 a.m. Monday to 4.0 a.m. Sunday	Marshals as required
		No. 2 Marshalling	6.0 a.m. Monday to 8.0 p.m. Saturday	„ „ „
		No. 3 Marshalling	8.0 a.m. to 1838 Down (SX) ..	7.15 p.m. Tinsley West to Broughton Lane (SX) : Marshals as required
			8.0 a.m. to 1824 Down (SO) ..	12.45 p.m. Tinsley West to Broughton Lane (SO) : Marshals as required
		No. 4 Marshalling	10.30 a.m. to 7.0 p.m. (SX) 10.0 a.m. to 3.0 p.m. (SO)	Marshals as required ⎫ Suspended. „ „ „ ⎬
FRODINGHAM, Trent Jct.	Frodingham	No. I Marshalling	10.0 p.m. Sunday to 6.0 p.m. Sunday	Marshals as required
New Yd. (Out'ds)	„	No. 2 „	10.0 p.m. Sunday to 6.0 p.m. Sunday	„ „ „
Works Ent. "A"	„	No. 3 „	10.0 p.m. Sunday to 6.0 p.m. Sunday	„ „ „
North Lincoln ..	„	No. 4 „	10.0 p.m. Sunday to 6.0 p.m. Sunday	„ „ „
Goods Yard ..	„	No. 5 „	6.0 a.m. to 10.0 p.m. Weekdays	„ „ „
Trent Down Sdgs.	„	No. 6 „	10.0 p.m. Sunday to 6.0 p.m. Sunday	„ „ „
New Yd. (Inw'ds)	„	No. 7 „	6.0 a.m. Monday to 6.0 p.m. Sunday	„ „ „
Transfers ..	„	No. 8 Transfers	10.0 p.m. Sunday to 6.0 p.m. Sunday	Transfer as required
North Lincoln ..	„	No. 9 Marshalling	3.0 p.m. Monday to Friday 3.0 p.m. to 11.0 p.m. Saturday only	Marshals and Transfers as required
Works Ent. " E "	„	No. 10 „	10.0 p.m. Sunday to 6.0 p.m. Sunday	Marshals as required
GRANGE LANE	Darnall ..	No. I Marshalling	7.0 a.m. to 3.0 p.m. Weekdays	Shunts Dropping Well Colliery. Depart Grange Lane 3.0 p.m, LE to Broughton Lane to work 6.13 p.m. Broughton Lane to Meadow Hall and 7.30 p.m. Chapeltown to Broughton Lane then LE to Shed.
HEXTHORPE ..	Doncaster ..	No. I Marshalling	6.0 a.m. to 10.0 p.m. Weekdays	Marshals as required. Suspended 10.0 p.m. to 6.0 a.m. Weekdays
	„ ..	No. 2 „	5.30 a.m. Monday to 6.0 a.m. Sunday	Marshals as required
Cherry Tree ..	„ ..	No. 3 „	6.0 a.m. Monday to 3.0 a.m. Sundays	Marshals as required.
Top Yard ..			8.30 p.m. (SX) to 5.30 a.m. (MX) 8.30 p.m. (SO) to 3.0 a.m. (Su)	Stand Pilot at Top Yard to 5.30 a.m. (SX) and 3.0 a.m. (Su), then to Cherry Tree to take up working at that point (SuX)
Hexthorpe Jct.	„ ..	No. 4 Banking and Travelling	8.0 a.m. to 9.0 p.m. Weekdays	Banking trains Hexthorpe Jct.: also works trains as follows :— Hexthorpe .. dep. 8.45 a.m. York Road .. arr. 10. 5 a.m. „ „ .. dep. 11.55 a.m. Hexthorpe .. arr. 12.27 p.m. Doncaster South Yard .. dep. 9.50 p.m. Hexthorpe .. arr. 10.20 p.m. „ .. dep. 12.50 a.m. Mexboro' .. arr. 1.19 a.m.
		No. 5 Marshalling	12.0 noon to 3.0 a.m. Weekdays..	Marshals as required and works trips to Top Yard, Decoy, and transfers between Hexthorpe Yards
KEADBY ..	Frodingham	No. I Marshalling	7.30 a.m. to 7.30 p.m. Weekdays	Marshals at Keadby Canal Jct. and shunts out at that place coal for shipment and works it to Keadby Goods for No. 3 Pilot to place in position. Shunt out wagons to be turned and for future requirements at the Jct. Shunt South Oil Works at 10.0 a.m. Weekdays. Leave Keadby Jct. 2.0 p.m. Weekdays unless otherwise instructed by the Station Master, to shunt Hart's Siding.
		No 2 Banking ..	6.0 a.m. Monday to 3.0 a.m. Sunday	Or until after passing of last Up Freight Train. Banking trains
		No. 3 Marshalling	6.15 a.m. to 6.15 p.m. Weekdays	Transfers traffic from Keadby Canal Down Sidings, placing into coal road 10 wagons at a time for contractors engine working into Power Station, and taking out empties as placed by contractors engine.

Station or Yard	Depot from which Engine provided	Number or description of Pilot	Period required at Station or Yard	Particulars of Work
MARSHGATE ..	Doncaster ..	No. 1 Marshalling	6.0 a.m. Monday to 6.0 a.m. Sunday	Marshal wagons from Yard and work traffic from Marshgate to Wheatley Park Branch Line and to Hexthorpe as required
MEADOW HALL	Darnall ..	No. 1 Marshalling	8.25 a.m. to 9.30 p.m. Weekdays	Marshals as required
MEXBORO' Goods Yard ..	Mexboro' ..	No. 1 Marshalling	6.0 a.m. Monday to 6.0 a.m. Sunday	Marshals as required
No. 2 Junction	,, ..	No. 2 ,,	5.0 a.m. Monday to 7.0 a.m. Sunday	Or after last train is disposed of. Marshals as required. On Sundays utilized in gassing stock and changing trains for cleaning purposes, etc.
Private Siding	,, ..	No. 3 ,, and Travelling	10.30 a.m. to 6.30 p.m. (SX) 9.30 a.m. to 5.30 p.m. (SO) ..	Marshals as required. Also works as follows :—

				p.m.
			Mexboro' No. 3 .. dep.	12.30
			Manvers Main Coll. arr.	1. 4
			,, ,, ,, dep.	1.35 EB
				p.m.
			Wath Yard .. .. arr.	1.43
			,, ... dep.	2.20
			Mexboro' No. 3 .. arr.	2.52

Station or Yard	Depot from which Engine provided	Number or description of Pilot	Period required at Station or Yard	Particulars of Work
NORMANBY PARK	Frodingham ,,	No. 1 Marshalling No. 2 ,,	10.0 p.m. Sunday to 6.0 p.m. Weekdays 4.0 a.m. to 8.0 p.m. Weekdays ..	Marshals as required ,, ,, ,,
NOTTON and ROYSTON	Barnsley ..	No. 1 Travelling	6.0 a.m. to 8.40 p.m. Weekdays..	Works as follows :—

				arr. a.m.	dep. a.m.
			Pindar Oaks ..	—	6.36
			Notton & Royston	7.12	7.29
					p.m.
			Monckton.. ..	7.34	6.15
			(Shunts Monckton Colliery)		
				arr. p.m.	dep. p.m.
			Notton & Royston	6.20	7.45
			Wh. Woodmoor	7.55	8. 5
			Smithies	8.15	8.25
			Pindar Oaks ..	8.45	

Station or Yard	Depot from which Engine provided	Number or description of Pilot	Period required at Station or Yard	Particulars of Work
ROTHERHAM & MASBORO'	Darnall ..	No. 1 Marshalling	{ 5.0 a.m. to 9.0 p.m. (MO) .. { 6.0 a.m. to 9.0 p.m. (MX) ..	Marshals as required. Shunts Rotherham Forge 12 noon to 1.0 p.m.
Ickles	,, ..	No. 2 ,,	12.35 a.m. Monday to 10.0 p.m. Sunday	Marshals as required at Ickles. Takes Locos 12 mdt. and returns to Ickles
,, ... Templeboro' ..	,, ..	No. 3 ,, No. 4 ,,	7.0 a.m. Monday to 7.0 p.m. Sunday 6.0 a.m. Monday to 10.0 p.m. Weekdays ..	Marshals as required at Ickles Marshals as required at Templeboro'
ROTHERHAM ROAD	Mexboro' ..	No. 1 Marshalling	1.0 a.m. Monday to 6.0 a.m. Sunday	Marshals as required. Changes over with engine working 8.44 a.m. Tinsley West to Don Bridge East.
STAINCROSS ..	Barnsley ..	No. 1 Travelling	7.0 a.m. to 8.0 p.m. Weekdays ..	Works :—Pindar Oaks dep. 7.0 a.m. ; Wharncliffe Woodmoor arr. 8.39 a.m. Then to instructions of S.M. Staincross until :— Smithies dep. 7.10 p.m. ; Barnsley arr. 8.0 p.m.
STAIRFOOT .. —	Barnsley .. ,,	No. 1 Marshalling No. 2 Travelling	5.0 a.m. Monday to 5.0 a.m. Sunday { 5.0 a.m. to 1.15 p.m. Weekdays { 1.15 p.m. to 8.10 p.m. Weekdays	Marshals as required Marshals as required at Stairfoot ; then works as follows :—

				SX	SO
			Stairfoot dep.	1.15 p.m.	12.40 p.m.
			Oakwell arr.	1.23 p.m.	12.45 p.m.
			,, dep.	1.34 p.m.	1.30 p.m.
			Old Mill arr.	1.39 p.m.	1.35 p.m.
			Lane		
			,, ,, dep.	2.30 p.m.	3.25 p.m.
			Oakwell arr.	2.35 p.m.	
			,, dep.	6.15 p.m.	
			Stairfoot arr.	6.28 p.m.	3.38 p.m.

Then assists No. 1274, 5.13 p.m. Grimsby to Ashton Moss from Stairfoot.

Station or Yard	Depot from which Engine provided	Number or description of Pilot	Period required at Station or Yard	Particulars of Work
	,, ..	No. 3 Marshalling	5.30 a.m. to 10.30 p.m. (SX) ..	Marshals as required and banks 9.40 p.m. Wath to Horbury then to shed
			5.30 a.m. to 11.30 p.m. (SO) ..	Marshals as required and banks 10.25 p.m. Wath to Barnsley then to shed

BOOKED SHUNTING ENGINES—continued.

Station or Yard	Depot from which Engine provided	Number or description of Pilot	Period required at Station or Yard	Particulars of Work
STAINFORTH ..	Doncaster ..	No. 1 Marshalling	6.0 a.m. Monday to 6.0 a.m. Sunday	Marshals as required
	,, ..	No. 2 ,,	6.0 a.m. Monday to 6.0 a.m. Sunday	,, ,, ,,
Thorne Jct. ..,	,, ..	No. 3 ,,	6.0 a.m. to 10.0 p.m. (MX) ..	Marshals as required. Also makes
			2.0 p.m. to 10.0 p.m. (MO)	trips between Thorne Jct. and Stainforth
SUMMER LANE	Barnsley ..	No. 1 Travelling	1.0 p.m. to 6.30 p.m. Weekdays..	Works as follows :— Barnsley .. .. | dep. 1. 0 p.m. Summer Lane .. | arr. 1. 9 p.m. (Shunts Sidings) | dep. 5.45 p.m. Barnsley Top Yd. | arr. 5.55 p.m. ,, ,, ,, | dep. 6.22 p.m. Pindar Oaks .. | arr. 6.30 p.m.
TINSLEY.. ..	Darnall ..	No. 1 Banking ..	3.20 a.m. Monday to 4.0 a.m. Sunday	Banking as required
		No. 2 ,,	3.0 a.m. Monday to 2.0 p.m. Sunday	
WARMSWORTH South	Doncaster ..	No. 1 Marshalling	7.25 a.m. to 8.40 p.m. Weekdays	Marshals as required and works between Warmsworth South and Yorkshire Main Colliery as required
WATH YARD "A" Hump ..	Mexboro' ..	No. 1 Marshalling	4.0 a.m. Monday to 10.0 p.m. Saturday	Marshals as required ⎤
"A" Hump ..	,, ..	No. 2 ,,	6.0 a.m. to 10.0 p.m. Weekdays..	,, ,, ,, ⎟
"B" Hump ..	,, ..	No. 4 ,,	4.0 a.m. Monday to 10.0 p.m. Saturday	,, ,, ,, ⎬ A
"B" Hump ..	,, ..	No. 5 ,,	6.0 a.m. to 10.0 p.m. Weekdays..	,, ,, ,, ⎟
Moor Road ,..	,, ..	No. 6 ,,	1.0 a.m. to 5.0 a.m. (MO) ..	⎥
			9.0 p.m. to 5.0 a.m. (SX)	⎦
"A" Hump ..	Mexboro' ..	No. 1 Marshalling	4.0 a.m. Monday to 12.0 mid Saturday	Marshals as required ⎤
"A" Hump ..	,, ..	No. 2 ,,	6.0 a.m. to 10.0 p.m. Weekdays..	,, ,, ,, ⎟
Banking ..	,, ..	No. 3 Banking ..	As required..	Banking as required ⎟
"B" Hump ..	,, ..	No. 4 Marshalling	4.0 a.m. Monday to 12.0 mid Saturday	Marshals as required ⎬ B
"B" Hump ..	,, ..	No. 5 ,,	6.0 a.m. to 10.0 p.m. Weekdays..	,, ,, ,, ⎟
Moor Road ..	,, ..	No. 6 ,,	1.0 a.m. to 5.0 a.m. (MO) ..	,, ,, ,, ⎥
			9.0 p.m. to 5.0 a.m. (SX)	⎦
	,, ..	No. 7 Travelling. .	6.30 a.m. Monday to Saturday to 2.30 a.m. Tuesday to Sunday	Works trips as required between Wath Yard and Manvers Main Colliery
	,, ..	No. 8 ,,	7.30 a.m. Monday to Friday to 1.30 a.m. Tuesday to Saturday 7.30 a.m. to 12.0 midnight Saturday	Works trips as required between Wath Yard and Wath Main Colliery

A—Applies April to November inclusive.   B—Applies December to March inclusive.

WORSBORO' BRANCH				
Garratt ..	Mexboro' ..	No. 1 Banking ..	6.0 a.m. Monday to 8.30 a.m. Saturday	Banking as required
8 W.C.	,, ..	,, ,,	8.30 a.m. Saturday to 2.0 a.m. Sunday	,, ,, ,,
8 W.C. ..	,, ..	No. 2 ,, ..	10.0 a.m. Monday to 2.0 a.m. Sunday	,, ,, ,,
8 W.C. ..	,, ..	No. 3 ,, ..	10.0 a.m. to 7.30 p.m. (MO) ..	,, ,, ,,
			4.0 a.m. to 7.30 p.m. (MX) ..	,, ,, ,,

Saturday, 5th May—*continued*.

No. 23.—Lincoln, Market Rasen, &c. to Hull and back.

(Wild West Show in Hull.)

		a.m.			p.m.
Lincoln	dep.	9 30	Hull (Packet)	dep.	7 45
Reepham	"	9 40	New Holland	arr.	8 5
Langworth	"	9 45	"	dep.	8 15
Snelland	"	9 51	Barnetby	"	8 40
Wickenby	"	9 55	Howsham	"	8 50
Market Rasen	"	10 5	North Kelsey	"	8 55
Usselby	"	10 12	Moortown	"	9 0
Holton	"	10 18	Holton	"	9 4
Moortown	"	10 22	Usselby	"	9 10
North Kelsey	"	10 27	Market Rasen	"	9 18
Howsham	"	10 82	Wickenby	"	9 27
Barnetby	arr.	10 42	Snelland	"	9 31
	dep.	10 46	Langworth	"	9 37
New Holland	arr.	11 11	Reepham	"	9 43
	dep.	11 20	Lincoln	arr.	9 52
Hull (Packet)	arr.	11 40			

Mr. CAINE, Lincoln, to provide Carriages, Roof Lamps (ready trimmed), and Guards.

Sheffield Locomotive Department to provide Power.

Mr. WELLS to provide Packet accommodation.

Tickets to be examined at Barnetby in going, and collected at the respective Stations on return.

Roof Lamps to be lighted at New Holland on return.

No. 24.—Penistone, Doncaster, &c. to Hull and back.

(Wild West Show in Hull.)

		a.m.			p.m.
Penistone	dep.	9 0	Hull (Packet)	dep.	8 15
Silkstone	"	9 10	New Holland	arr.	8 35
Dodworth	"	9 16	"	dep.	8 45
Barnsley	"	9 25	Barnetby	pass	9 13
Stairfoot	"	9 32	Elsham	dep.	9 20
Wombwell	"	9 38	Appleby	"	9 29
Wath	"	9 45	Frodingham	"	9 37
Mexboro'	"	9 52	Gunness	"	9 46
Conisboro'	"	9 58	Althorpe	"	10 0
Doncaster	"	10 10	Crowle	"	10 8
Barnby Dun	"	10 20	Thorne	"	10 20
Stainforth	"	10 26	Stainforth	"	10 27
Thorne	"	10 83	Barnby Dun	"	10 33
Crowle	"	10 45	Doncaster	arr.	10 42
Althorpe	"	10 53		dep.	10 45
Gunness	"	10 56	Conisboro'	"	10 55
Frodingham	"	11 4	Mexboro'	"	11 1
Appleby	"	11 12	Wath	"	11 8
Elsham	"	11 21	Wombwell	"	11 15
Barnetby	arr.	11 27	Stairfoot	"	11 22
	dep.	11 32	Barnsley	"	11 30
New Holland	arr.	11 57	Dodworth	"	11 38
	dep.	12 5	Silkstone	"	11 44
Hull (Packet)	arr.	12 25	Penistone	arr.	11 54

Mr. HODKINSON, Sheffield, to provide Carriages, Roof Lamps (ready trimmed), and Guards, and

Sheffield Locomotive Department to provide Power.

The Empty Train to leave Sheffield for Penistone at 7-45 a.m.

Tickets to be examined at Barnetby in going, and collected at the respective Stations on return.

Doncaster Tickets to be collected at Barnby Dun, and Barnsley Tickets at Stairfoot.

Mr. WELLS, Hull, to provide Packet accommodation.

Roof Lamps to be lighted at New Holland on return.

ES/PT

B1413/98

THE ~~RAILWAY EXECUTIVE~~   **BRITISH RAILWAYS**   DISTRICT GOODS SUPERINTENDENT
EASTERN REGION   Claims Section
                                                     BRIDGEHOUSES GOODS STATION
                                                         SHEFFIELD, 3

Tel: ~~Mex~~ 25051 .   Ext.   15.   Ref. XA.15178.   Date   5th November 1953.

To . Goods Agent,
     WHITWELL.   Reference

Engine 48176 in collision with 12.45 a.m. "J" Leeds –
Masboro' Up Goods Line, Houghton, 4.35 a.m. 30.10.53.

Please note the enclosed extract from a letter received from
the Leeds D.G.S. concerning a collision at Houghton, and advise me if any
claim is lodged.

From.	To.	Wagon No.	Contents.	Label date.	Remarks.
Perth	Whitwell	159964	Potatoes	27.10.53.	Contents transhipped into wagon 50202 (8 bags burst) sent forward 2.11.53
Perth	Whitwell	79471	Potatoes	27.10.53.	Thrown over parapet of rail bridge into river. Not yet salvaged.
Forres	Whitwell Colly.	92719	Pit Props	26.10.53.	Contents transhipped into wagons 494140 and 450265 and sent forward 2.11.53.

for R.B. Temple.

RETURN

FROM

LEEDS

(CENTRAL)

at 10-20 p m

FOR

WAKEFIELD

(WESTGATE)

FITZWILLIAM

HEMSWORTH

UPTON AND
NORTH ELMSALL

KIRKSMEATON

301 SPCL 28 2.53

Related works by the same author:
'The Dearne Valley Railway.'
'The GN and GE Joint Railway.'
'The Railways of North Lincolnshire.' (reprinting)

NOTES

NOTES

NOTES